*This book was purchased
with funds from a
generous donation by*

Dr. Kathryn W. Davis

Amy Poehler

by Stephanie Watson

LUCENT BOOKS

A part of Gale, Cengage Learning

GALE
CENGAGE Learning·

Detroit • New York • San Francisco • New Haven, Conn • Waterville, Maine • London

LIBRARY OF CONGRESS CATALOGING-IN-PUBLICATION DATA

Watson, Stephanie.
  Amy Poehler / by Stephanie Watson.
    pages cm. -- (People in the news)
  Includes bibliographical references and index.
  ISBN 978-1-4205-0883-3 (hardcover)
  1. Poehler, Amy, 1971---Juvenile literature. 2. Actors--United States--Biography--Juvenile literature. I. Title.
  PN2287.P565W38 2013
  792.702'8092--dc23
  [B]
                                                      2013028261

Lucent Books
27500 Drake Rd.
Farmington Hills, MI 48331

ISBN-13: 978-1-4205-0883-3
ISBN-10: 1-4205-0883-0

Printed in the United States of America
1 2 3 4 5 6 7 17 16 15 14 13

Contents

Fame and celebrity are alluring. People are drawn to those who walk in fame's spotlight, whether they are known for great accomplishments or for notorious deeds. The lives of the famous pique public interest and attract attention, perhaps because their experiences seem in some ways so different from, yet in other ways so similar to, our own.

Newspapers, magazines, and television regularly capitalize on this fascination with celebrity by running profiles of famous people. For example, television programs such as *Entertainment Tonight* devote all their programming to stories about entertainment and entertainers. Magazines such as People fill their pages with stories of the private lives of famous people. Even newspapers, newsmagazines, and television news frequently delve into the lives of well-known personalities. Despite the number of articles and programs, few provide more than a superficial glimpse at their subjects.

Lucent's People in the News series offers young readers a deeper look into the lives of today's newsmakers, the influences that have shaped them, and the impact they have had in their fields of endeavor and on other people's lives. The subjects of the series hail from many disciplines and walks of life. They include authors, musicians, athletes, political leaders, entertainers, entrepreneurs, and others who have made a mark on modern life and who, in many cases, will continue to do so for years to come.

These biographies are more than factual chronicles. Each book emphasizes the contributions, accomplishments, or deeds that have brought fame or notoriety to the individual and shows how that person has influenced modern life. Authors portray their subjects in a realistic, unsentimental light. For example, Bill Gates—cofounder of the software giant Microsoft—has been instrumental in making personal computers the most vital tool of the modern age. Few dispute his business savvy, his perseverance, or his technical expertise, yet critics say he is ruthless in his dealings with competitors and driven more by his desire to maintain Microsoft's dominance in the computer industry than by an interest in furthering technology.

In these books, young readers will encounter inspiring stories about real people who achieved success despite enormous obstacles. Oprah Winfrey—one of the most powerful, most watched, and wealthiest women in television history—spent the first six years of her life in the care of her grandparents while her unwed mother sought work and a better life elsewhere. Her adolescence was colored by pregnancy at age fourteen, rape, and sexual abuse.

Each author documents and supports his or her work with an array of primary and secondary source quotations taken from diaries, letters, speeches, and interviews. All quotes are footnoted to show readers exactly how and where biographers derive their information and provide guidance for further research. The quotations enliven the text by giving readers eyewitness views of the life and accomplishments of each person covered in the People in the News series.

In addition, each book in the series includes photographs, annotated bibliographies, timelines, and comprehensive indexes. For both the casual reader and the student researcher, the People in the News series offers insight into the lives of today's newsmakers—people who shape the way we live, work, and play in the modern age.

Changing the Course of Comedy

In the 1970s if people wanted to laugh at comedy, chances are the jokes came from a man. Men dominated the world of comedy at the time: George Carlin, Cheech Marin and Tommy Chong (known as Cheech and Chong), Richard Pryor, and Bill Cosby made up most of the funny faces people saw when they turned on their televisions.

When the comedy/variety series *Saturday Night Live (SNL)* launched in 1975, it featured funny men like Chevy Chase, John Belushi, and Dan Aykroyd. The show was groundbreaking in that it combined comedy sketches with political satire and musical acts. Yet the show also introduced something relatively new—female comedians who could be just as bold and unapologetically funny as their male counterparts. For example, the original cast of *SNL* featured actress Gilda Radner, who played a range of characters, from nerdy Lisa Loopner to ranting news commentator Roseanne Roseannadanna. Radner was fearless in the way she boldly broke into the boys' club of comedy to become a star of late-night television.

Welcome to the Girls' Club of Comedy

In the late 1970s a little girl in the suburbs of Boston was avidly watching Radner's rise to fame. Her name was Amy Poehler. Like Radner, Poehler was gifted with a quick wit, a sharp tongue, and a fearless stage presence. Even in elementary school she was not afraid to get on stage and perform. By the time she was in high school, she was acting in school plays. In college, she put her stage presence and comedy talents to work in improvisational comedy (improv).

Poehler eventually made her own name in comedy, playing characters on the same show that had made Radner famous. Beyond just making people laugh, Poehler helped form a girls'

Amy Poehler pursued her childhood dreams of performing and made them a reality.

club of comedians. Along with actresses like Rachel Dratch and Tina Fey, Poehler created female characters that helped reinvigorate *SNL* and proved that women could be just as funny as, if not funnier than, men.

Competing in a Man's Industry

In part because she had role models like Radner, and because her parents encouraged her to be whatever she wanted, Poehler has never been afraid to compete in a male-dominated and often cutthroat industry. She has attacked comedy head-on, which is a lot to say for someone who stands just five feet two inches tall. "When you're short and blond and a woman in comedy, you get underestimated," Poehler says. "I *love* being underestimated."[1]

Much of Poehler's comedy has centered on another male-dominated field—politics. She earned her reputation on *Saturday Night Live* reporting the mock news on the "Weekend Update" segment. She became famous for her impression of presidential candidate Hillary Clinton during the 2008 election, an impression that Clinton herself reportedly loved. In fact, one of the most memorable moments during Poehler's time on *SNL* came during that presidential election.

It was October 18, 2008, just weeks before the historic vote. Republican vice presidential candidate Sarah Palin, the governor of Alaska, was scheduled to appear on the show. There was much controversy surrounding Palin since she was brought in as presidential candidate John McCain's running mate relatively late in the campaign, and many questioned her ability and expertise as a vice presidential candidate. With fumbled answers to interviewers' questions and mockable misinformation about important domestic and foreign policy issues, Palin became routine fodder for comedy shows like *SNL,* which took many shots at the candidate.

A "Meaningful Moment for Women"

Despite the jokes at her expense, Palin agreed to appear on "Weekend Update" to do a rap battle with Poehler. But at the last minute Palin got cold feet, so Poehler stepped up and agreed to do the entire rap by herself. Poehler, who happened to be nine-months pregnant at the time, delivered a hard-core rap that she had personally written. Backing her up were two dancers dressed as Eskimos and an actor in a snowboarding outfit who was supposed to be Todd Palin, Sarah's husband. From behind the news desk, she rapped, "McCain got style, but don't let him freak you out when he tries to smile. Because that smile be creepy, but when I be VP, all the leaders in the world gonna finally meet me. . . . My country tis a thee, from my porch I can see, Russia and such. All the mavericks in the house put your hands up!"[2]

While Poehler rapped away next to her, Palin, who still appeared on the show even though she bowed out of performing the rap, gamely bopped along to the music. Regardless of her

In one of Poehler's most memorable "Weekend Update" skits, she raps a song about 2008 vice presidential candidate Sarah Palin while Palin (right) plays along.

own political stance or opinion about the election, Poehler tried to be respectful toward the candidate. She wanted to have fun without being overly mean or insensitive to Palin, whom Poehler thought was brave to appear on the show. She appreciated that Palin was such a good sport about the whole thing.

For many who watched the episode, rapping in front of Sarah Palin, especially while nine-months pregnant, was an impressively bold move. They considered it an important point in a very divisive political campaign. In fact, Poehler's friend and former *SNL* costar Fey called it "the most meaningful moment for women in the 2008 campaign."[3] Fey and others thought a three-minute skit poking fun at political candidate Palin on "Weekend Update" might possibly have changed the course of the entire election, by parodying Palin's views on important issues such as foreign affairs and energy production.

A Most Influential Person

Poehler's campaign rap was just one of many meaningful moments in what has become a very memorable career. After leaving *SNL*, she helped to create one of the most successful sitcoms on network television, *Parks and Recreation*. She has been nominated for Emmy, Golden Globe, MTV Movie, and Writers Guild Awards. In 2011 she was honored as one of *Time* magazine's "100 Most Influential People on the Planet." She has also strived to make comedy with a message, as evidenced by her decision to launch her own cartoon show and website to foster self-esteem and individuality in preteen girls.

Over the years, Poehler has worn many different guises. She has played everything from little girls in braces to politicians in suits. Yet despite the variety of characters she has portrayed, Poehler has never lost touch with who she is. Friends and coworkers claim that she is one of the nicest people in show business, without a trace of celebrity ego. She has also never forgotten where she got her start, as a little girl with big dreams in a working-class Massachusetts town.

Chapter 1

Boston Born
and Bred

L ong before she was coanchoring the news desk on *Saturday Night Live* or trying to beautify a fictional town on *Parks and Recreation*, Amy Poehler was just a kid growing up in the Boston suburb of Burlington, Massachusetts. "Boston has a scruffiness to it, a blue-collar work ethic that I can relate to. You have to be able to take it on the chin and keep proving yourself,"[4] Poehler says of her hometown. Add to that strong work ethic a good sense of humor, and it becomes clear that Poehler is a product of her environment. "Bostonians don't take themselves too seriously, and they don't let anyone else take themselves too seriously,"[5] she says. Poehler has often been praised for the same work ethic and sense of humor she admires so much in others.

The Poehler Family Tree

Amy Meredith Poehler was born on September 16, 1971. When she was three years old, younger brother Greg arrived. Their parents, Bill and Eileen Poehler, had met while in college. Bill was captain of the basketball team, and Eileen was captain of the cheerleading squad. They both went on to become teachers, with Bill teaching elementary school math and Eileen teaching high school special education.

Like many people who have lived for generations in New England, the Poehler family tree has long roots in the region. Poehler has a Nantucket, Massachusetts, ancestor in common

Poehler's parents, Bill and Eileen (pictured here far left and far right, with Poehler's then husband Will Arnett, in 2008), knew from an early age that young Amy was comfortable performing on stage and supported her in doing so.

with *Moby Dick* author, Herman Melville. Founding Father Benjamin Franklin is her first cousin (although they are separated by ten generations, which makes them ten times removed). She also shares genes with former vice president Dick Cheney and U.S. senator from Massachusetts Scott Brown. These influential bloodlines may have something to do with her natural proclivity for political comedy.

Growing Up 1980s Style

Amy grew up in Massachusetts during the 1980s, a time when everything seemed big, including linebacker-sized shoulder pads and sky-high hair. She once described growing up near Boston during the 1980s like living out the lyrics to a Bon Jovi song: "Big hair, big dreams, but safe."[6]

Years later, her childhood memories would take shape in a 2007 *SNL* skit called "Amy's Bedroom," in which she poked fun at the decade and at her middle-class upbringing. She even got

Famous Bostonians

Amy Poehler is among many famous people who hail from Boston. A number of other notaries from the worlds of entertainment, literature, and politics have also called Beantown and its surroundings home, including:

- John Adams: This Founding Father and second U.S. president was born and practiced law in Braintree (now Quincy).

- John F. Kennedy: The thirty-fifth U.S. president grew up in a house on Beals Street in Brookline, a wealthy Boston suburb.

- George H.W. Bush: The forty-first president came from posh suburban Boston digs, the well-heeled town of Newton.

- Mark Wahlberg: The former rapper known as Marky Mark, who is now an Academy Award–nominated actor and producer, started out as a tough kid from Dorchester.

- Brian Noonan: This New York Ranger probably slapped his first hockey puck in his hometown of South Boston.

- John Krasinski: Long before he starred in the NBC hit sitcom *The Office*, Krasinski spent his days in Newton, Massachusetts. His former costar, Steve Carell, also hails from the Boston area.

- Edgar Allan Poe: The author who delivered chills with *The Raven* and other spooky stories was born on January 19, 1809, in Boston.

- Donna Summer: Before she became known as the queen of disco, Summer discovered her voice in Boston, where she was known as LaDonna Adrian Gaines.

- Jane Curtin: She was born in nearby Cambridge, Massachusetts, but Curtin became famous in New York as one of the original cast members on *Saturday Night Live*.

a little help from rocker Jon Bon Jovi himself. The skit is set in a pretend version of her teenage bedroom, where a big-haired Amy is writing in her diary. (Yearbook photos confirm that Amy's hair reached soaring heights back in high school.) The teenaged Amy complains in a thick Boston accent about being

Poehler as a senior at Burlington High School in 1989.

teased at school (although Amy seemed to be well-liked at her own high school) and having a "wicked bad" life ("wicked" is a Boston slang word that means "very").

Suddenly, Bon Jovi steps out of a poster on her wall and promises the struggling teen that a brighter future lies ahead. "I got some pretty big dreams," she tells him. "I don't wanna just *shop* at the Limited, I wanna *work* at the Limited!"[7] Bon Jovi assures her she is destined to do something much bigger than work at the mall. He tells her that one day, she will be a cast member on *Saturday Night Live*.

An Outgoing, Good Kid

In real life, Amy was much more confident than the character she played in "Amy's Bedroom." As one school episode illustrates, she had no fear of getting up on stage in front of an audience. "Once, in the fourth grade, the principal was on stage and he had the mike up high," her father remembers. "Then little Amy walks across, goes up to the mike, grabs the little knob, twists it, pulls it down, and I said to myself, 'Oh my God, she has no stage fright whatsoever.'"[8] Amy had boundless energy and a limitless view of her own potential, qualities that she would years later give to characters like Kaitlin and Bessie Higgenbottom.

At Burlington High School, Amy had a lot of friends and was involved in many different activities, from student council to cheerleading. "I did drama, but I also did sports, so I hung out with all different crowds," she says. "I really liked school because my parents were public school teachers. I was a good kid."[9]

When she and her friends were not hanging out at the Burlington Mall (where she jokes that she practically grew up), Amy held a few odd jobs. She waited tables at Chadwick's, an ice cream parlor in the nearby town of Lexington. "We wore Styrofoam hats and we had to sing and dance when it was somebody's birthday,"[10] she remembers. Interestingly, fellow *Saturday Night Live* star Rachel Dratch worked there a few years before Amy, although the two did not meet until they worked together on the show.

At an early age, Amy became active in politics. She helped her father pass out flyers for town council meetings. Amy even took part in the 1988 presidential campaign of former Massachusetts governor Michael Dukakis, the Democratic nominee. Although Dukakis did not win the election, Amy learned a lot about the political system by working for him.

"When in Doubt, Go Crazy"

As a child, Amy was as funny as she was feisty. She brimmed with confidence and energy. "I was a big-time ham," she remembers. Her father claims she inherited her now-famous sense of humor from him. Being just one member of an all-around funny family meant "you had to hold your own at our table,"[11] she says.

Ever the jokester, Amy did not shy away from pulling pranks at home. One Christmas Day, when Amy was told she and her brother were not allowed to get up until 6:30 A.M. to open presents, she snuck through the house and turned all the clocks back three hours so that everyone had to wake up at 3:30 A.M. instead.

Amy also flaunted the silly side of her personality at school. In the fifth grade, she and a friend handcuffed themselves to each other and then somehow managed to lose the key. Her mother recalls, "The principal called me and said, 'Mrs. Poehler, there's been a mishap.'"[12] These and other pranks earned her a reputation for having a high-energy zaniness in high school. As a result, friends nicknamed her "crazy Amy" and "Poehlercoaster."

Amy honed her comedic instincts by watching some of the great funny men and women on 1970s television. She loved the physical humor of comedy duo Penny Marshall and Cindy Williams on their sitcom *Laverne & Shirley*. The character of Archie Bunker, the grumpy blue-collar dad on *All in the Family*, rang true to her. She says Animal, the wild drummer on *The Muppets*, taught her that "when in doubt, go crazy."[13] From Animal, she may have also gotten the urge to play the drums, which she listed as her "secret desire" in her high school yearbook.

In high school Poehler (second row, second from right) was involved in many extracurricular activities, including cheerleading.

One of her favorite comedians at the time was *SNL* star Gilda Radner. Amy admired her in part because she worked so easily with all of the male comedians around her. "I remember when I was a kid watching Gilda and saying, 'All the guys look like they really like her. Everybody looks like they really want her to be around,'"[14] she says.

Amy Onstage

Even in childhood, Amy's passions for acting and comedy were clear. She loved acting out fairy tales, only she preferred to play the male hero rather than the maiden who needed rescuing. "I liked Cinderella and Snow White, but what I really liked was the action of doing things like riding on horses and saving people,"[15] she says.

In high school, Amy tried to get into dramatic plays, but it was hard to hide her true gift. "I kept going out for serious roles and getting cast for comic relief. I wanted to be the brooding, complicated brunette, but I guess that wasn't me,"[16] she admits.

Amy was funny, smart, and quick on her feet—perfect attributes for comedy. Realizing her talents, her high school theater

Gilda Radner

One of Amy Poehler's heroes was Gilda Radner, who in the 1970s was one of the reigning queens of TV comedy. As an original member of the 1975 *Saturday Night Live* cast, she created unforgettable characters, like whiny news anchor Roseanne Roseannadanna, and Baba Wawa, a parody of real reporter Barbara Walters.

Radner was born in 1946 in Detroit, Michigan. She studied theater at the University of Michigan but never graduated. In 1973 she joined the Second City theater troupe in Toronto, Canada (fellow comedic actors Dan Aykroyd, John Belushi, and John Candy were also members). While there, she caught the attention of TV producer Lorne Michaels, who was working on developing a late-night comedy show for NBC. He was so impressed that he hired her, and she became a regular on *Saturday Night Live* from 1975 to 1980.

In 1984 Radner married comedy actor Gene Wilder. Just two years later, she was diagnosed with ovarian cancer. She died on May 20, 1989, shortly before her forty-third birthday. Despite her short life, she remains one of the most respected female comedians in the history of television.

Gilda Radner was a pioneer for women in the world of comedy.

coach in the late 1980s cast her as Princess Winnifred, the lead role in the school's production of *Once upon a Mattress*, a musical comedy based on the Hans Christian Andersen fairy tale "The Princess and the Pea."

When Amy graduated from Burlington High in 1989, one of her relatives, without realizing it, predicted her future comedy career. Her aunt gave her a graduation card that read, "I'll see you on *Saturday Night Live*."[17]

Finding Humor in College

By the end of high school, Amy was more than ready to move on and start working toward her future. "I remember at the end of my senior year in high school, I wasn't at all interested in attending my graduation," she says. "I just kept thinking, 'I need to get out of here! What's next?'"[18]

After graduating from Burlington High School, Amy did not go far. She went to Boston College, a large liberal arts school in nearby Chestnut Hill, Massachusetts. At first, she signed up as a communications major, and her parents thought she was destined to become a reporter. For a while, Amy did consider becoming a writer, or perhaps a teacher like her parents. But then she joined Boston College's improv troupe, My Mother's Fleabag, and her direction changed completely.

Made up solely of students, My Mother's Fleabag is the oldest college-based improvisational troupe in the country. (Improv is a type of comedy in which the performers make up routines as they go along, usually following suggestions from the audience.) Since 1980 My Mother's Fleabag has performed in many different venues throughout the Boston area. Each semester ends with one "Big Show" at Boston College's O'Connell House. The group builds a stage on which they perform sketches, games, and an opera—all made up entirely on the spot. The actors interact with the audience to flesh out a humorous sketch or a game. For example, one popular Fleabagger game is called "185 Blanks." After asking the audience for a noun, the troupe members use it to improvise a joke that starts, "185 [noun]s walk into a bar. . . ."

While attending Boston College, Poehler got her first taste of comedy when she joined the school's improv group, My Mother's Fleabag.

"Different in All the Right Ways"

When Amy joined My Mother's Fleabag, she immediately felt right at home. "I was kind of overwhelmed when I went to BC [Boston College] by the homogeneity," she said. "I was surrounded by rich prep-school kids, and I didn't come from that world. Fleabag was filled with the kind of strange and beautiful and crazy people who were different in all the right ways."[19] She was hooked.

After graduating from Boston College in 1993, Amy announced to her family that she wanted to perform improv comedy for a living. Her family had always supported her and encouraged her to pursue her dreams, and this time was no exception, or so it seemed to Amy. According to her father, he and her mother told her, "Oh, that's great. Do whatever makes you happy, honey." Then they walked into another room, looked at each other, and said, "Oh my God! We just spent all that money and now she's going to be an actress?"[20]

Comedic acting might not have seemed to Amy's parents like the ideal profession, especially for a smart girl with an expensive college degree, but it was clearly her passion. During the next few years, Amy would put her comedic instincts to the test. She quickly discovered that breaking into the comedy business was a lot harder than just getting a few laughs.

Chapter 2

An Upright Citizen

In her early twenties, Amy Poehler had her heart set on a career in improvisational comedy. Yet talent and ambition alone were not enough to propel her to success. It would take many years of hard work, including launching a comedy troupe from the ground up and performing in small venues for little or no money, before she was finally able to make a name for herself in the world of comedy.

Go West, Young Comedian

Fresh out of college with a degree and some basic improv training, Poehler headed west to Chicago, Illinois. "Chicago, like a lot of cities, was in an early-nineties depression. A lot of flannel, a lot of good music, a lot of bad politics,"[21] she jokes of the area at the time.

Though it was not an entertainment hub like New York City or Los Angeles, Chicago had earned a reputation for comedy. This was largely due to the Second City and Improv Olympic, two comedy troupes that form the foundation of Chicago's improvisational comedy.

The Second City is the older of the two groups. Since 1959 it has introduced dozens of famous comedians, including former *Saturday Night Live* stars Gilda Radner, Dan Aykroyd, and John Belushi. Improv Olympic has only been in existence since 1981, but it also has a legendary cast of actors on its roster, including Mike Myers, Andy Richter, Chris Farley, and Tim Meadows.

Poehler took classes with both groups and was grateful for the training. At Improv Olympic, she studied under legendary

To hone her improv and comedy skills, Poehler joined the famous Second City troupe in Chicago, similar to the one in Los Angeles advertised here.

TAKE A CLASS

ACTING • IMPROVISATION • WRITING
MUSIC • DIRECTING

improv coach Del Close. He had helped launch the careers of Belushi, Bill Murray, and Radner. "I've never really met or talked to somebody who's actually invented something that I care about so passionately," she says of her mentor. "I really do feel like he invented pretty much what we're all doing."[22]

From her college improv troupe, Poehler had brought with her to Chicago a slow, gradual approach to improv. The scenes were long and took time to develop. At Improv Olympic and the Second City, she learned a faster, more aggressive comedy style. Poehler also learned how to play with her fellow comedians onstage. She has compared improv to being on a basketball team "and knowing when to pass and knowing when to shoot."[23]

The Beginning of an Important Friendship

While at Improv Olympic, Poehler met Tina Fey, a self-described nerd who had found a way to put her dorky style and intelligence to work in improv comedy. It was love at first sight. "I was like, I finally found the woman I want to marry,"[24] Poehler teases.

Their dedication to their craft showed. "They were just instantly brilliant," Charna Halpern, cofounder of Improv Olympic, says of Poehler and Fey. "They were not the typical women who get steamrolled by men. [They] were no shrinking violets."[25]

Poehler met and formed a longstanding friendship with fellow comedian Tina Fey, seen here in 2006, while both were taking comedy classes in Chicago in the 1990s.

Their unique styles of comedy (Poehler's humor was silly, while Fey's was biting) worked well together. The pair's instant chemistry created a powerful bond both on- and offstage. "They were inseparable,"[26] says Kelly Leonard, executive vice president at Second City. Poehler and Fey became close friends very quickly, but professionally, they were about to part ways. Fey was offered a job in New York, writing for *Saturday Night Live*, while Poehler stayed in Chicago just a little while longer.

Upright Citizens Brigade

While Poehler honed her improv technique with two of the most established troupes in Chicago, elsewhere in town a fledgling group was just finding its comedy voice. The Upright Citizens Brigade (UCB) began in 1991 as a loose group of improv and sketch comics, most of whom, like Poehler, had studied under Close. Many of the group's early members, who included Matt Besser, Matt Walsh, Ian Roberts, Horatio Sanz (who later joined the cast of *SNL*), and Ali Farahnakian, rotated, revolving door-like, in and out of UCB.

One thing could be said about the members of UCB, they were not afraid to try anything. In one early skit, Sanz staged a street

Second City

When Amy Poehler came to study at Chicago's Second City improv troupe, the group had already been in existence for more than thirty years. Founded in 1959, the Second City was based on the work of Viola Spolin, who is considered the mother of improvisational theater.

The groundbreaking comedy group became a household name in the 1970s, when its graduates started moving on to bigger venues. John Belushi, Dan Aykroyd, and Gilda Radner headed to *Saturday Night Live*. John Candy, Eugene Levy, and Rick Moranis emerged from the Second City's spin-off group in Canada to become big movie stars in the United States. Some later well-known graduates include Steve Carell, Stephen Colbert, and Tina Fey. In 2009 the Second City celebrated its fiftieth anniversary.

protest and was really arrested. To his acting credit, Sanz stayed in character, even while the officer was cuffing him and pulling him into the police car. "After the car pulls away, I'm like, 'I'm an actor, by the way.' I spent the night in jail,"[27] Sanz recalls.

After Poehler joined UCB in 1995, the group was cemented as a foursome: Poehler, Besser, Walsh, and Roberts. The three men eagerly welcomed a female member into their fold. Being on stage surrounded by three experienced improv comedians, all of them men and all over six feet tall, might have intimidated some women, but not Poehler. "She controls the scene, and never takes the backseat or plays a typical sort of role as women do to themselves sometimes, to choose to play the girlfriend or something like that," Ian Roberts comments. Instead, Poehler played quirkier characters, like a talkative Girl Scout who befriends the Unabomber. "She's completely as dominant as anybody onstage," notes Roberts. "You'd never say, 'she's funny for a girl,'"[28] he adds.

Although she could not even reach her fellow actors' hands to high-five them before shows, Poehler always held her own on stage. "She's an alpha performer," says her later fellow *SNL* cast member Seth Meyers. "I think that's ingrained in her, but it got trained very well, being with those other three guys."[29]

The UCB foursome managed to somehow be funny, gross, crazy, and smart all at the same time. They often pulled crazy stunts, such as dressing one of their members up as Santa Claus and filming him as he stood outside a toy store offering alcohol to children (New York police officers who came upon this particular scene did not find it humorous). The four formed a bond so tight that it came across when they were onstage. "UCB is part high school, part rehab, part training camp, part substitute family, part junior college for life, and you have to figure out how to manage this high school without anybody blowing it up,"[30] Poehler says. The "high school" part included at least one romantic hookup: Poehler and Besser began dating, but the relationship did not last long.

Taking Big Swings

By 1996 the four members of UCB felt it was time to expand their comedy horizons. They thought they could gain more

The four core members of the Upright Citizens Brigade (from left to right, Matt Besser, Poehler, Ian Roberts, and Matt Walsh) getting silly at a 2013 performance.

of a following in a bigger city; namely, New York. Although they were young and inexperienced, they were very ambitious. "Moving to New York and trying to get a show—oh my God, we were naïve," Poehler recalls. "But the great thing about taking big chances when you're younger," she adds, "is you have less to lose, and you don't know as much. So you take big swings."[31]

It was a big swing, but it would not be a miss. Although the city was already full of stand-up comedy clubs, improv troupes were surprisingly lacking, especially groups doing long-form comedy (full-length shows) like UCB. Poehler packed her entire belongings into a U-Haul truck, and she moved from a five-hundred-dollar-a-month apartment in Chicago to a nine-hundred-dollar-a-month studio (one-room apartment) in New York City.

UCB began performing at clubs such as Rebar and Luna Lounge, where edgy comedians like Janeane Garofalo and Louis C.K. frequently did stand-up. UCB was not a hit right away. Some

Upright Citizens Brigade

Amy Poehler was just one quarter of the four-person improv comedy troupe known as Upright Citizens Brigade. She shared the stage with Matt Besser, who graduated from Amherst College in Massachusetts and traveled to the Midwest to study with Del Close at Improv Olympic. In addition to founding UCB, he has had his own one-man show and has launched programs for MTV, Comedy Central, and TBS. In recent years, he has guest-starred on several hit TV shows, including Poehler's own *Parks and Recreation*.

Ian Roberts hails from Secaucus, New Jersey. In 1990 he moved to Chicago to tour with Second City. Since helping found UCB, Roberts has performed in every show the group has done. He's also acted in movies, including *Bring It On* with Kirsten Dunst and *Anchorman: The Legend of Ron Burgundy* with Will Ferrell.

Matt Walsh helped launch UCB theaters in New York and Los Angeles, where he still performs and teaches. In 2001 he served as a correspondent for the satirical news program *The Daily Show with Jon Stewart* on Comedy Central. Walsh has also acted in dozens of movies and TV shows, including *Old School*, *Starsky & Hutch*, and *Role Models*.

nights, only a handful of people were in the audience. The four UCB members would try to scrounge up more audience members by passing out flyers in Greenwich Village's Washington Square Park. They would promote their shows through a bullhorn to get the attention of people passing by. "We got a lot of weirdos at our shows and very small audiences,"[32] Poehler recalls.

Dreaming Big

UCB performed some of their shows for free, just to get attention. At each show, they would put a piece of tape across the backs of a few seats in the audience and write the word "HBO" across them.

They hoped that executives from that cable network might stop by to see the show and be so impressed they would offer UCB its own TV show. But HBO executives never showed up.

The group's lack of immediate success did not bother Poehler. She did not have an issue with paying her dues. In some ways, she even found the image of the starving artist appealing. "There's something so romantic about being broke in New York. You gotta do it,"[33] she quips.

UCB created four separate improv shows, which they performed in various clubs. In one of the shows, one actor would take an idea from the audience and build a story out of it. Then the rest of the troupe would make up skits based on that story. What made UCB unique was that it could put a bizarre twist on the most boring, mundane stories. Often, one member of the group would sit in the audience. Once the show started, he or she would interrupt the show by pretending to be an invented, crazy character, such as a drunk racist or an angry obstetrician.

By night, UCB would perform; during the day, the members would make extra money by teaching improv classes. Their "school" was a tiny, forty-seat theater space called the Solo Arts Group in the Chelsea neighborhood of New York. Once UCB had gained a small following, however, they outgrew this tiny theater and built their own, bigger venue on West Twenty-Second Street in Chelsea. The Upright Citizens Brigade Theatre opened on February 4, 1999. It quickly became one of the most respected sketch-comedy clubs in the city.

Creating Chaos

Soon it was time to think bigger than the small stage. The group had one overriding goal: to land a television deal. Luckily, Kent Alterman, vice president of programming at the Comedy Central network, thought UCB was the perfect alternative to the same old sketch-comedy shows that filled network time slots in the late 1990s. He appreciated the troupe's "unyielding and darkly comedic"[34] sensibility. Comedy Central not only picked up *Upright Citizens Brigade* in 1998, but the network put the show in its coveted Wednesday 10:30 P.M. time slot, following the hugely popular *South Park*.

In the show's opening sequence, UCB described itself as a "secret organization" whose mission was to "find chaos where it exists . . . and create chaos where it does not."[35] Each episode was based on a scene that would build and build, spinning more and more out of control with each passing minute. In one show, a real estate agent showed a family around a house they were interested in buying. It seemed innocent enough, until the real estate agent opened the door to the "hot chicks room," filled with beautiful women who partied all day long. Then the daughter (played by Poehler) jumped a fence and befriended the Unabomber, a wanted terrorist, who was living next door.

Another episode featured a fake commercial selling a CD called *Honest Rock*—songs performed by musicians who "refuse to conform to the beauty standards of the music industry."[36] Among those musicians was a singer-songwriter, played by Poehler covered in werewolf-like fur, and a pianist with an exposed spine. On the series Poehler often assumed the personalities of dozens of different characters, from an angry bus driver to an overly earnest teen with a speech impediment.

Upright Citizens Brigade found its following on TV, just as it had in New York comedy clubs. Yet the ratings were not high enough for Comedy Central to commit to renewing it further. The network canceled the show in 2000, after a three-year run. Despite their disappointment, the cast kept their sense of humor. "It was too good," Poehler jokes. "Comedy Central couldn't keep it because the show was . . . making the other shows look bad."[37] There was more bad news to come.

UCB Expands

In November 2002, the UCB Theatre was shut down for a fire-code violation. For nearly a year, the group was homeless. Losing their venue did not deter the four actors, though. They performed wherever they could find space around the city until they were able to secure a new location.

Finally, on April 1, 2003, UCB opened a new, 150-seat theater on West Twenty-Sixth Street. Just two years later they expanded, branching out to the West Coast with a new theater

Although Poehler has a successful acting career, she is proud of her improv roots and still performs with her fellow Upright Citizens Brigade members whenever possible, such as in this 2011 performance with Horatio Sanz (left) and Matt Walsh (right).

in Hollywood, California. In its theaters, UCB opened improv training centers. Today, about eight thousand students take classes at its New York and Los Angeles locations. The classes offered in both locations range from the basics of improvisation to sketch-comedy writing and how to turn a funny idea into a full-blown comedy sketch. An eight-week class costs $350. Some of the classes are so popular that they sell out within a minute after opening for registration.

Poehler calls the creation of UCB's theaters "by far my proudest professional accomplishment." She marvels that the small group was able to have such a far reach. "We were just a group from Chicago," she says, "trying to get a TV show and an agent and have people notice us."[38] Even when she had moved on to doing television and movies, Poehler always returned to her roots on the stage, performing regularly in UCB's shows. "Going and performing at the theater is kind of a relief," she says. "It's pretty easy to do something that fun with people that talented."[39]

As UCB's recognition grew on both coasts, it became harder and harder to find an open seat at the group's shows. Many of those seats were filled with casting directors and agents. They began offering the talented performers television and movie roles, especially Poehler. "Some of us had opportunities to make money [by] splitting up the group. We fought that off for a while," Poehler says. "Every once in a while, a sitcom would come up, and I didn't torture myself by putting myself in the position to get things and then have to turn them down."[40]

A Chance to Be Young Again

Eventually, though, Poehler was offered a few roles that she could not turn down. One of them was a part in *Wet Hot American Summer*. The 2001 film was a parody of summer camp movies from the 1970s and 1980s. Poehler plays an overzealous musical director named Susie at fictional Camp Firewood.

Poehler played opposite some then relatively unknown actors who have since gone on to huge success, including Bradley Cooper, Christopher Meloni, and Elizabeth Banks. The atmosphere on set was a lot like the camp life they were portraying. "While it was happening, I knew I would probably never have this much fun working on a movie again," says Poehler, who had never had a chance to go to summer camp in real life. "It was getting to go back to your adolescence in your 30s, but knowing all you know and having your party skills refined."[41]

Wet Hot American Summer earned only $300,000 at the box office, but it became an instant cult classic. It had such lasting power that in 2012, the cast reunited to perform a live radio play of the movie at the Marines' Memorial Theatre in San Francisco.

In the late 1990s Poehler also had a repeating cameo role on the "Conan O'Brien Show" as sidekick Andy Richter's little sister Stacy. The pigtailed, brace-faced tween would pop up from time to time in the audience to express her massive, obsessive crush on O'Brien. Soon, another popular late-night TV show would offer Poehler her first really big break.

Chapter 3

Live from New York!

Just about every comedic actor's dream is to showcase his or her talents on a network program like *Saturday Night Live*. Amy Poehler was about to get her biggest break yet, but her debut could not have come at a worse time in the show's history.

A Dream Gig

While living and working in New York City with UCB, Poehler got to know many of the local comedians. A few of her friends were regular cast members on *Saturday Night Live* (*SNL*), the late-night NBC comedy variety show. For comedic actors, *SNL* is a dream gig. Since the 1970s the show has earned a reputation for turning unknown talents into television and movie stars. John Belushi, Adam Sandler, Dana Carvey, Chevy Chase, Jimmy Fallon, Bill Murray, Molly Shannon, and Tina Fey are just a few of the big names who got their start on *SNL*. Poehler grew up watching the show, and she has called it "the best comedy training ground on television."[42] Finally, she got the chance to work in that training ground.

In an appearance on CNN's *Larry King Live* Poehler joked about how she got cast on the show. "I just met [creator/producer] Lorne [Michaels] in an undisclosed location and I handed him an envelope filled with $50,000 and here I am."[43] In reality, she was asked to audition just like any other *SNL* hopeful, and Michaels gave her the opportunity of a lifetime when he hired her.

Finding Comedy amid Terror

Poehler joined the cast of *SNL* on September 29, 2001. It was a very dramatic episode, the first one that aired after the terrorist attacks of September 11. On that day, nineteen terrorists hijacked four planes above the United States. They crashed two planes into the World Trade Center in New York City and one into the Pentagon in Washington, D.C. Passengers on the fourth plane were able to wrest control from the terrorists, crashing their plane into a field in Pennsylvania rather than into its intended target (likely somewhere else in the District of Columbia). In all, about three thousand people were killed, and the attacks launched both the war in Afghanistan and the war on Terror (including the war in Iraq).

With the entire country in mourning, it was not the ideal time for Poehler to make her TV comedy debut. "You're just trying to figure out where the bathrooms are, and on top of it, everyone's like, 'Will comedy be able to go on?' If you didn't feel small and insignificant before, you definitely did then,"[44] she says.

To acknowledge what the nation had been through, Michaels started the show with a tribute song for New York's police and firefighters, performed by music legend Paul Simon. Then he asked New York mayor Rudy Giuliani for his permission to be funny again. "Why start now?"[45] the mayor quipped in response. The joke got a big laugh, and the cast, including Poehler, knew they had the mayor's, as well as the entire country's permission to be funny again.

Nevertheless, they proceeded with caution during those first few shows after 9/11. They skirted around political humor, sticking to the types of skits they knew would take Americans' minds off their grief. In her monologue at the opening of that first post-9/11 show, host Reese Witherspoon explained, "We've never done a show under these circumstances, so we're still finding our way. But I promise you that we're gonna give it everything we've got."[46]

In the second show that season, Will Ferrell did a sketch highlighting the country's increased patriotism in the wake of the terrorist attacks. In the skit, he wore a tiny American-flag Speedo swimsuit and a cutoff T-shirt to work to show his patri-

Poehler's debut on Saturday Night Live *came just weeks after the 9/11 terrorist attacks. This skit from October 6, 2001, among others, helped bring humor back to a very dark time in American history.*

otism. He kept bending over his coworkers, revealing his backside in the very skimpy bathing suit. Sketches like these helped Americans laugh through their grief during those first difficult months after the attacks.

Kaitlin, Amber, and a Cast of Crazy Characters

When Poehler started on *SNL*, she joined a cast that included Rachel Dratch, Ana Gasteyer, Ferrell, Darrell Hammond, Chris Kattan, and Tracy Morgan. Seth Meyers, another young comedian who had started at Chicago's Improv Olympic, joined the cast at the same time as Poehler. Another show regular was Fey, who was thrilled to be working with her old friend again. "Weirdly, I remember thinking, 'My friend is here! My friend is here!' Even though things had been going great for me at

Saturday Night Live

Saturday Night Live, or *SNL* for short, has been making audiences laugh for more than three decades. Yet it started simply as a way to fill an empty Saturday late-night time slot on NBC. In 1974 producer Dick Ebersol turned to comedy writer Lorne Michaels for help in finding a show that could air in that 11:30 P.M. slot.

Once in charge, Michaels decided to take his show in a very different direction than the comedy variety shows that were airing at the time. He wanted something edgier, a show that would appeal to young adults. Michaels wanted his new series to really push the boundaries of comedy.

He pulled together some of the top comedy writers at the time and hired a cast he selected from two famous comedy troupes, the Second City in Chicago and the Groundlings in Los Angeles. That first cast, which was known as "The Not Ready for Prime Time Players," included Chevy Chase, Dan Aykroyd, John Belushi, Jane Curtin, Gilda Radner, Laraine Newman, and Garrett Morris. Each week's ninety-minute show featured a different celebrity guest host and musical act.

On October 11, 1975, at 11:30 P.M., *Saturday Night Live* premiered. In the years since then, *SNL* has created a huge cast of famous characters, from Martin Short's Ed Grimley, to Dana Carvey's The Church Lady, and Rachel Dratch's Debbie Downer. Today, the show is still going strong.

the show, with Amy there, I felt less alone,"[47] Fey writes in her memoir, *Bossypants.*

SNL has an established process for recruiting new talent. Usually, new cast members start out on the show as featured players. Then they either work their way up to regular cast members within a couple of years, or they get fired from the show. Poehler took the fast track, however. By Christmas 2001 she was already a full cast member. Only two other cast members had ever been promoted mid season—Eddie Murphy and Harry Shearer.

For much of its history, *SNL* had been a boys' club. Male comedians, including Dan Aykroyd, Belushi, Billy Crystal, and Ferrell, dominated the show. When Poehler joined *SNL*, she helped start a girls' club, along with Fey, Maya Rudolph, and Dratch. Together, the girls of *SNL* breathed new life into the series. "As any true blue fan of *Saturday Night Live* can tell you, over the past decade, it's been all about the ladies," writes *Entertainment Weekly* journalist Aly Semigran. "From Tina Fey to Maya Rudolph to Amy Poehler, the women of *SNL* all but dominated the laughs on the long-running series."[48] The trio of comedians, along with Dratch and Kristen Wiig, created a whole ensemble of unforgettable characters, including the always-morose Debbie Downer (played by Dratch), an over-the-top version of singer Whitney Houston (Rudolph), and the strange 1960s singer Dooneese (played by Wiig).

The show's female standouts did not just perform comedy. They ensured that they got the best lines by writing the show's skits themselves. "During the past few seasons, [head writer] Fey

Poehler playing "Kaitlin," one of her memorable **Saturday Night Live** *characters.*

has seen to it that the female performers (Amy Poehler, Rachel Dratch, and Maya Rudolph) play recurring, center-stage parts," notes journalist Virginia Heffernan. "Poehler and Dratch also write prolifically, often in collaboration with the staff writers Emily Spivey and Paula Pell."[49]

Poehler developed an entire collection of memorable characters, some famous, some soon-to-be famous. There was the hyperactive tween Kaitlin, who drove her Uncle Rick (played by Horatio Sanz) crazy. With her lisp, brimming confidence, and overeager personality, Kaitlin bore an uncanny resemblance to the Stacy character Poehler had played on Conan O'Brien's show and to the little girl who had befriended the Unabomber on *Upright Citizens Brigade*. Poehler has said that Kaitlin was a tribute to her idol, Gilda Radner. In the 1970s Radner had created a similarly geeky, gawky, super-hyper character named Judy Miller on *SNL*. Kaitlin also reflected Poehler's own childhood personality. "When I was that old, I was a little wound up myself," she admits. "I like that age, where you're not quite into boys yet and really think you can be an astronaut, a teacher, a doctor, and a roller skater. That girl and I live in the same world."[50]

She also created Amber, an overconfident, one-legged reality show contestant who appeared on shows like *America's Next Top Model* and *The Swan*. Another Poehler favorite was a character named Netti Bo Dance, a shuffling redneck in a housedress who visited the Appalachian Emergency Room along with her husband, Percy (played by Hammond). There was also Sally Needler, one-half of a couple (with Meyers) that could never stop arguing.

Poehler also perfected dozens of celebrity takeoffs, including Avril Lavigne, Sharon Osbourne, Paula Abdul, Anna Nicole Smith, and CBS News reporter Katie Couric. Not all of her characters were female, though. She also spoofed some male characters, such as North Korean dictator Kim Jong Il, Michael Jackson, and Project Runway–winning fashion designer Christian Siriano.

Political Humor

Probably Poehler's most memorable celebrity characterizations were neither actors nor musicians but politicians, including

Poehler's impersonation of former First Lady Hillary Clinton—seen here with Darrell Hammond impersonating former president Bill Clinton—garnered her a lot of attention, and a lot of laughs.

Hillary Rodham Clinton. When playing Clinton, Poehler did not try to copy the former First Lady exactly. Instead, her version was a blend of personality traits that people associated with Clinton, especially her determination to become president and her frustration with the political race. "I don't look like Hillary or sound like her, so I had to come up with another way to come at the character," Poehler says. "I made the game of playing Hillary more about her having to grit her teeth through debates with [then Democratic presidential contender Barack] Obama or appearing with [Republican vice presidential nominee] Sarah Palin."[51]

She gave Clinton a cackling laugh that sounded nothing like the then senator's real laugh. "But that laugh came from her trying to keep things down and kind of not being able to believe all the stuff that she had to deal with,"[52] Poehler explains. The way she played Clinton during the 2008 election allowed even

people who were not familiar with the candidate to find something to laugh at in the character.

Clinton had a good sense of humor about Poehler's portrayal
of her. She even came on the show and raved, "I simply adore
Amy's impression of me." Just then, Poehler emerged on set
wearing the exact same outfit and hairstyle. As the two identical
Clintons came face-to-face, Poehler gushed, "I love your outfit."
To which Clinton replied with a smile, "Well, I love your outfit.
But I do want the earrings back."[53]

"Much-Needed Oxygen"

Some of Poehler's funniest moments on *SNL* came during the
2008 presidential election, when she played Clinton to Fey's
dead-on impression of vice presidential nominee Palin. While
Fey (as Palin) preened for the camera, Poehler's Clinton com-

*Tina Fey (left) as Sarah Palin and Poehler as Hillary
Clinton was one of the top pop culture highlights of the
2008 presidential election.*

plained, "I don't want to hear you compare your road to the White House to my road to the White House! I scratched and clawed through mud and barbed wire, and you just glided in on a dog sled wearing your pageant sash and your Tina Fey glasses!"[54] In another sketch as Clinton, Poehler hilariously asked Americans to stop treating her as a sex symbol.

In one of her best-known performances on the show, a nine-months pregnant Poehler delivered a bold rap about Palin on "Weekend Update." Poehler unabashedly delivered lines that made fun of Palin's gaffes, policy initiatives, and personal habits all while Palin was sitting right next to her.

Although these skits were primarily meant to be funny, they were taking jabs at real politicians. In a very tight race, some political commentators thought Fey and Poehler might have influenced the election by poking fun at Palin's views on important issues and making her seem inexperienced or uninformed. Even though the presidency went to Obama and running mate Joe Biden, the election greatly enhanced Clinton's political standing and ensured her a top spot in Obama's cabinet (she was eventually named secretary of state, a position in which her reputation soared further). "Amy Poehler's impersonation of Hillary Clinton on *Saturday Night Live* will be remembered as one of the high points of the 2008 election," one reporter writes. "It also managed to steer the political debate, lure Clinton onto *SNL*—excavating her sense of humor in the process—and give her campaign some much-needed oxygen."[55]

An Over-the-Top Style

Whether playing out-of-control celebrities or passionate politicians, Poehler has never been afraid to take her characters over the top to get laughs. "I think she's fun to watch because she's best at the comedy of joy—her characters always seem to be having more fun than anyone else,"[56] Meyers says. She has also avoided getting stereotyped into cutesy or sexy feminine roles. Fey agrees, and praises Poehler for creating and pursuing characters that are front and center. "Amy made it clear that she wasn't [at *SNL*] to be cute," writes Fey in *Bossypants*. "She wasn't there to play wives and girlfriends in the boys' scenes. She was there to do what she wanted."[57]

In an industry obsessed with looks, it is noteworthy that Poehler has never been afraid to play unattractive characters. She has hooded her eyes with a unibrow, stuck moles on her chin, and even put on a full mustache and beard. For Poehler, comedy comes before beauty. "Amy is this beautiful girl, but she'd as soon wear goofy teeth and fright wigs,"[58] explains Fey. In fact, one of the only places on *SNL* where Poehler actually appeared as her attractive self was at the "Weekend Update" desk.

"Weekend Update"

"Weekend Update" is one of the most famous segments on *SNL*. This mock-news skit pokes fun at politicians, recent events, and people who have been in the news that week. It has become the show's longest running skit and continues to be one of its most popular segments.

Anchoring "Weekend Update" is a particularly demanding job. To make sure the jokes are as up-to-date as possible, the writing for the segment is always done last, sometimes just hours before the show airs. From 2000 to 2004 Fey and Fallon were coanchors. The pair developed an easy rapport during their time together behind the news desk. When Fallon announced at the end of the 2004 season that he was leaving the show, *SNL*'s producers knew they had to find someone who could match his chemistry with Fey. "It was a big decision because 'Update' has always been the thing that speaks for the show,"[59] said producer Michaels.

Fey wanted her longtime friend for the recurring role, and Michaels agreed that Poehler was a natural choice. He liked Poehler's energy, her fearless approach to comedy, and her easy relationship with Fey. They were the perfect coanchors for the skit. When they premiered together on October 2, 2004, Poehler and Fey became the first all-female news duo in the show's history. Poehler describes her excitement at being chosen for the coveted spot, "I feel like—like—a blushing bride." Fey jumps in, adding, "And I feel like an older, Greek oil magnate who's

"Weekend Update"

Often controversial and always hilarious, "Weekend Update" has been part of *SNL* since its first season. Over the years, several members of the ensemble cast have taken their turns behind the news desk.

Chevy Chase launched "Weekend Update" as its first anchor. He started off each segment with the memorable line, "Good evening, I'm Chevy Chase, and you're not." Other notable anchors were Jane Curtin (1976–1980), Dan Aykroyd (1977–1978), Kevin Nealon (1991–1994), Norm Macdonald (1994–1997), Jimmy Fallon (2000–2004), and Tina Fey (2000–2006).

Many of the show's regulars, along with some guests, have made appearances on "Weekend Update." Adam Sandler dramatically sang the news as Opera Man in the mid-1990s. Whitney Houston showed up a few times (actually, it was Maya Rudolph doing her hilarious impression of Houston). And Gwyneth Paltrow once walked onto the set to plant a few kisses on Jimmy Fallon, while a surprised Tina Fey looked on.

Quoted in Saturday-Night-Live.com. "Weekend Update Through the Years." www .saturday-night-live.com/history/weekendupdate.html.

taken a young bride. Secretly, she's disgusted by me but she has no choice."[60] She was referring to Aristotle Onassis, the wealthy shipping tycoon who married the much younger Jacqueline Kennedy in 1968.

Being in a regular sketch boosted Poehler's status on the show as well. For the first time, the audience heard her name on a weekly basis. Poehler also said that anchoring "Weekend Update" helped loosen her up so she could perform better in her other skits.

Behind the Anchor's Desk

As cohosts of "Weekend Update," Poehler and Fey made sure no topic was off limits. In one segment, they poked fun at twin actresses Mary-Kate and Ashley Olsen, who had been accused of producing their clothing line in an overseas sweatshop (a factory where workers, many of them children, are employed at very low wages and work in very poor conditions). They also poked fun at Bill O'Reilly in the same segment, showing their disdain for the conservative news commentator with a graphic screen that labeled him disgusting.

In another episode, Poehler and Fey announced that for the holiday season they had volunteered to be part of the Teen Mentoring Program of America. Then they announced which teen they would be mentoring—Lindsay Lohan. Poehler and Fey proceeded to grill Lohan (who had recently been called out by the press for being too thin and getting into trouble) about her diet and career, much to Lohan's mock embarrassment.

"Really!?!"

In 2006 it was Tina Fey's turn to leave *SNL*. When Fey moved on to her NBC sitcom *30 Rock*, *SNL*'s head writer Meyers slid easily into the seat she had vacated. Michaels said he chose Meyers because he and Poehler had had good chemistry as "the Needlers," the recurring couple who argued all the time.

The two took their partnership one step further, launching a segment called "Really!?!" that poked fun at hot topics and political foibles. In their first segment, which launched during the 2006/2007 *SNL* season, they pointed the finger at football player Michael Vick, who had recently gotten into trouble for trying to carry drugs onto an airplane. As they recounted the ridiculous story of how Vick got caught, they asked over and over again, "Really!?!"

In another memorable "Really!?!" skit, from 2008, the target of their humor was Illinois governor Rod Blagojevich, who had recently been arrested on corruption charges. First Poehler and Meyers focused on the political trouble the governor was in. Then they targeted his hair. "It looks like you're wearing a toupee that's also wearing a toupee," said Poehler. "It's like you have a pro-ceeding hairline,"[61] Meyers added.

The "Weekend Update" pairing of Poehler and Seth Meyers, seen here doing one of their "Really!?!" segments in 2007, was a success for several seasons of Saturday Night Live.

Of all the people Meyers has worked with on *Saturday Night Live*, he says Poehler was the most fun to be around. "She's like everything wrapped into one. She's a bit of a cheerleader, a quarterback, class president [and] class clown. She's kind of a force of nature comedy-wise."[62] Meyers and Poehler were the perfect comedy pair, but soon it would be time for them to part, as well.

An Emmy and a Good-Bye

Winning an Emmy Award is one of the highest honors any television actor can receive. It means that your peers see you as one of the most talented actors or actresses on television. It is as big an achievement as winning an Academy Award is to a film actor. In the past, ensemble members on variety shows like *SNL* were not eligible to be nominated for individual Emmys, but a shift in the rules changed that in 2008, and Poehler became the first person on *SNL* to ever be nominated. She was nominated for the Outstanding Supporting Actress in a Comedy Series award.

The episode that earned Poehler the nomination contained a who's who of Poehler characters, including Clinton. She ended up losing the Emmy to Jean Smart from *Samantha Who?*, surprising many industry insiders who had predicted that Poehler would win.

The year that earned Poehler her first Emmy nod was her seventh season on *SNL*. Though she was dedicated to the show, it was not the only focus of her life. She was pregnant with her first child with husband, actor Will Arnett. In addition, she had

Poehler, as a first-time Emmy nominee, and husband Will Arnett attend the Primetime Emmy Awards in 2008.

just been offered the lead role in a new NBC sitcom under development. It was time to move on to the next stage of her career.

Poehler said an emotional good-bye to the cast and crew during a "Weekend Update" segment. "I did just want to take a moment to thank everybody. This is my last show, and it has been an amazing experience to be here," she said. "Being able to do over 140 shows with my friends and my family has been a dream come true."[63]

When she was interviewed three years later, Poehler had nothing but fond memories of her time on *SNL*. "I miss the immediacy of it," she said. "I miss something happening in the news on a Friday and then scrambling to update a sketch."[64]

Poehler did return to *SNL* a few times to host. In September 2010 she helped kick off the show's thirty-sixth season. In February 2012 she rejoined former "Weekend Update" cohost Meyers to revive the "Really!?!" segment. They pointed the finger at the Republican presidential candidates and their political views. She even took part in a "Weekend Update Joke-Off," where she and Meyers went up against Fey and Fallon to see who could come up with the funniest punchline (Fey and Fallon won).

Still, it was time for Poehler to move on. She had made her mark on *SNL* with a whole family of unforgettable characters, some real, some straight out of her imagination. Now it was time to focus on her own family and to push her career even further with a sitcom created just for her.

Chapter 4

Baby Mama

The year 2008 was important to Amy Poehler for several reasons. It was the year she left *SNL* to pursue her own sitcom. It was also the year in which she was nominated for her first Emmy Award and gave birth to her first child. But before becoming a mama in real life, Poehler played one on screen.

A Different Kind of Comedy

Shortly after launching her show, *30 Rock,* Tina Fey turned her attention back to moviemaking. She was interested in making a different, unique kind of comedy, one that featured two female leads. She knew that Poehler was exactly the female she wanted to play opposite.

In *Baby Mama,* Fey plays Kate Holbrook, a successful businesswoman in her late thirties who yearns for a child. Because she has spent so much of her life focused on her career, Kate now faces serious fertility issues. To realize her dream of having a baby, she hires an obnoxious, gum-chomping, working-class woman, Angie Ostrowiski (played by Poehler), to be a surrogate mother (a woman who carries an already fertilized egg to term in her womb for someone else).

The movie was notable for the way in which Poehler and Fey formed what some critics described as a new, female version of the *Odd Couple* (the 1960s film and 1970s TV sitcom about two male roommates who are complete opposites). Holbrook is the buttoned-up professional businesswoman, while Ostrowiski is the rough-around-the-edges working-class girl.

To illustrate the characters' differences, in one scene, Ostrowiski takes her chewing gum out of her mouth and sticks it right to the bottom of Holbrook's expensive-looking coffee table. This prompts Holbrook to ask, "Do you think you're at an Arby's right now?"[65] In another scene, Holbrook catches Ostrowiski peeing in the bathroom sink because she is unable to figure out how to open the toilet seat, which has been childproofed. To Holbrook's horrified expression, Ostrowiski responds casually from her perch on the sink, "There's something wrong with your toilet."[66] The vast personality differences between the two women contribute to these and many other awkward yet funny moments in the film.

Baby Mama was a unique addition to the comedy offerings of the time, for several reasons. For one, it was unusual to see a comedy featuring two female leads. Many of the other popular comedies in theaters at the time, such as *Superbad, Knocked Up,*

The 2008 comedy **Baby Mama** *reunited offscreen friends Poehler and Tina Fey.*

or *Forgetting Sarah Marshall,* were directed by men, featured male leads, and portrayed dilemmas and events from a male perspective. Females are part of the story, but largely as supporting characters or tangential figures. In fact, the genre of "buddy comedies" typically revolves around male friendships and groups.

Los Angeles Times film critic Peter Brownfield was impressed that in *Baby Mama* Poehler and Fey were able to carry a buddy comedy by themselves, and he appreciated seeing a funny story told from not just one female perspective, but two. "It seems unusual—if not illegal—for two females . . . to have the leads in a buddy comedy," he wrote. "It's almost like an experiment in comedy science class: What if [instead of to men] these roles went to funny women who've earned their shot at big-screen success?"[67]

"Taking Back Control of Their Profession"

Another unique aspect of *Baby Mama* was the way in which it covered a delicate, serious subject matter that might not seemingly lend itself to humor. Infertility often causes heartbreak for women and their families and is therefore not a funny topic. In that sober reality, Fey and Poehler found a welcome challenge. In fact, Fey says the universality and seriousness of the subject matter was a chief reason she was drawn to the script. "I liked the topicality of the fertility issues that affect so many people. There's so much weirdness and emotion about it. If you start with something juicy, you end up with a better [movie] than if you just start with some jokes."[68]

Despite its many positive attributes, *Baby Mama* received mixed reviews. "The film never comes fully to term, as it were: the visual style is sitcom functional, and even the zippiest jokes fall flat because of poor timing," wrote *New York Times* reviewer Manohla Dargis, even though she noted it "pulls you in with a provocative and, at least in current American movies, unusual mix of female intelligence."[69] Another reviewer called the film "an essentially sweet-natured picture that doesn't go as far as it could."[70]

No matter what they thought of the movie, however, almost all reviewers complimented Poehler and Fey for achieving a fe-

In Baby Mama Fey and Poehler brought humor to the serious subject of infertility.

male comedy team unique to contemporary cinema. "Though the competition hasn't exactly been stiff, Fey and Poehler may well be the best female comedy duo since Lucy and Ethel,"[71] wrote Claudia Puig in *USA Today*, referring to the characters played by Lucille Ball and Vivian Vance in the 1950s series *I Love Lucy*. Wesley Morris of the *Boston Globe* agreed: "In this era of . . . men monopolizing movie comedy, *Baby Mama* feels absurdly momentous, and even political. Fey and Poehler aren't just taking back control of their bodies. They're taking back control of their profession."[72]

Reporters also found much to praise in Poehler's physical comedy, which was on full display in *Baby Mama*. Poehler's Angie expresses horror at taking prenatal vitamins, eating healthy food, and drinking water; she also parades around in an enormous pregnant belly, feigning disgust at birthing classes and breast pumps, all the while performing eyebrow-raising antics in Poehler's classic over-the-top-style. "She's a pip . . . a nonstop, joyfully watchable whirligig," said Dargis in the *New York Times*. "If Angie works at all, it's because Ms. Poehler puts

Poehler Onscreen

Amy Poehler is probably best known for her movies *Baby Mama* and *Mean Girls*. Yet she has acted in a long list of films over the years. In 2004 she appeared in *Envy* as Jack Black's wife, Natalie Vanderpark. This movie is about two best friends who suddenly earn a fortune. Coincidentally, *Envy* opened in theaters on the same day as *Mean Girls,* but it did not do nearly as well.

In 2006 she appeared in *The Ex* as Carol Lane, coworker of Tom Reilly (Zach Braff) and Chip Sanders (Jason Bateman), two advertising agency employees who are fighting over the same woman. The following year she had a small part in *Mr. Woodcock* (2007). This film centers on John Farley (Sean William Scott), a writer who tries to persuade his mother (Susan Sarandon) not to marry his evil junior high school gym teacher (Billy Bob Thornton). Poehler plays John's book publicist. She portrayed a different kind of professional in *Hamlet 2* (2008); she was lawyer Cricket Feldstein in this movie about a high school theater teacher who puts on a very unusual version of William Shakespeare's play to save his school's drama program. Poehler was also featured in 2009's *Spring Breakdown,* which centers on three thirtysomething women who try to relive their youth during a spring break vacation.

a sweet spin on her character's gaffes, whether she's yelping in horror at the unfamiliar taste of water or squatting in a sink when nature makes an untimely call."[73]

A Tried-and-True Partnership

As always, reviewers also liked Poehler's comfortable partnership with Fey. During press interviews, it was easy to tell the women had been friends for years by the way they easily bounced jokes off each other. "The tiny babies were very professional, I must say," Poehler remarked to one reporter about the infant actors in the movie. "They had really teeny tiny baby trailers. Their demands weren't excessive, either. I need something to eat. I need something to drink." Then Fey jumped in, saying, "Milk and a nap. That's about it." Poehler finished with the punchline, "Now their toddler agents, *they* were annoying."[74]

Poehler and Fey had developed that rapport over nearly two decades of working together, first in Improv Olympic and then on *Saturday Night Live*. They had also worked together in an earlier movie, *Mean Girls*. The 2004 film, which Fey wrote, is about a teenager named Cady Heron (played by Lindsay Lohan) who tries to fit in with the nasty popular girls (called "The Plastics")

Poehler had a small but memorable role in the 2004 movie **Mean Girls.**

at her new high school. Fey plays Ms. Norbury, a teacher who tries to help the school's girls shed their cliquey habits and superficial ways. Poehler had a small part as a vain, overly girlish mother who desperately wants to be viewed as a "cool mom" by her daughter, head Plastic Regina George (played by Rachel McAdams). At the time, Poehler was only seven years older than McAdams, which at first made Poehler and Fey wonder whether Poehler was too young for the role. "I play a mom and Tina plays a teacher in it, and we were talking about how we didn't think we looked old enough to be the mothers of teenage girls," Poehler says. "Then Lindsay [Lohan] walked by, and we looked at her dewy, 17-year-old skin, then we looked at our skin and we immediately realized that actually, we do."[75]

Comedy Couple

Fey is not the only costar with whom Poehler has bonded over the years. In 2000 she met Canadian actor/comedian Will Arnett. Although Poehler jokes that they met through a Jewish dating site, in reality they were introduced by friends. They hit it off and were married three years later, in August 2003 (though their marriage ended in 2012).

When they were together, Poehler and Arnett made their relationship seem effortless, possibly because they both have such a strong sense of humor. "She's funnier than most dudes I know,"[76] Arnett said of his wife. Their easy relationship translated onto the screen during the few times the pair worked together. In 2004 and 2005 Poehler guest-starred as Arnett's wife in a few episodes of his Fox network series *Arrested Development*. In the 2007 movie *Blades of Glory*, they played a villainous brother-and-sister skating duo, Stranz and Fairchild Van Waldenberg. "It was nice to spend our off-time together," Poehler said of their film and TV partnerships and joked that working with her husband was also nice because "our parents are very pleased they only have to go to one movie."[77]

Comedian/actor Ben Stiller, who produced *Blades of Glory*, testified to the couple's easy working relationship: "It's fun to see their rhythm together, they play off each other so well. Will plays

Then real-life husband Will Arnett costarred with Poehler as her onscreen brother/skating partner in the 2007 comedy Blades of Glory.

things straight but with an awareness of what's funny. Amy is so good and polished as a live performer and has a funny, quirky sensibility."[78] The pair worked so well together, in fact, that they were compared with legendary husband-and-wife comedy duo Jerry Stiller and Anne Meara (who are Ben Stiller's parents).

Yet as Poehler's star has risen, Arnett sometimes found himself in his wife's shadow, even though at six feet two inches, he towers a full foot over her. In 2004, for example, a hotel concierge referred to him as "Mr. Poehler." Arnett tried to keep a sense of humor about his wife's success, although he admitted that at the time of that incident, "Amy laughed a little harder than I did."[79]

Aside from their work projects, it was often hard for Poehler and Arnett to find time alone together. That was especially true

Learning to Skate

Preparing for Poehler's role in *Blades of Glory* involved more than just memorizing lines and blocking (going to your spot on the stage). She also had to learn how to ice skate, which she had never done before. "I had never, ever skated," she says. "Zero experience. We had to take lessons, but I was probably the worst. I really was. Will [Arnett] is Canadian, and they come out of the womb with skates on."

To get good enough to play an ice-skating competitor, Poehler spent months taking both ballet and ice-skating lessons. She studied under former Olympic ice dancer, Judy Blumberg. Every morning, Poehler would meet Blumberg at Chelsea Piers in New York for her lesson before heading off, exhausted, to *Saturday Night Live* rehearsals. Although she was not transformed into a world-class competitive skater, Poehler did learn to navigate the ice well enough to pull off the part.

Quoted in Donna Freydkin. "Arnett & Poehler Sittin' in a Tree L-a-u-g-h-i-n-g; 'Glory' Stars' Marriage Is Anything but Icy." *USA Today*, March 23, 2007, p. E1.

during the early years of their marriage. They spent much of their time apart, working on opposite coasts. They lived in Manhattan, where *SNL* is filmed, but Arnett had to fly back and forth to Los Angeles to shoot *Arrested Development*. Their bicoastal marriage meant they had to carve out moments together whenever they could. "When we have a night off, we just fuel up our private jets, and we get up in the air and we stare at each other through each other's private-jet windows. Then we land and we have separate caviar dinners on our own private island,"[80] Poehler once joked to a reporter.

Poehler said her life with Arnett was far from exotic and not nearly as hilarious as people would imagine it to be. When they were able to find time together, they usually spent it having a quiet dinner with friends or sitting home on the couch watching

TV. Like other couples, they bickered over mundane tasks, like who should walk the dog. "I wish I could tell you that we had these crazy comedy competitions of hilariousness, but at the end of the day, all I want is a good cry and an hourlong drama,"[81] says Poehler.

Mama in Real Life

After playing a mother in the movies and meeting a man who was her comedic equal, Poehler was finally ready to have a child of her own. In the spring of 2008 she and Arnett announced that they were expecting a baby the following fall.

For many women, being pregnant brings a roller coaster of emotions, and this was no different for Poehler. She told a reporter that her pregnancy made her cry at everything. "The wind will blow a branch and I'm like, aw, nature."[82] In addition to her turbocharged emotions, trying to play different characters on *SNL* while sporting a huge belly was not easy. "Being pregnant and doing comedy is like wearing a giant sombrero in every scene," she says. "Everyone is just trying to pretend it's not there. It can be limiting."[83]

In late October, just hours before she was supposed to appear on *SNL*, Poehler went into labor. "Weekend Update" coanchor Seth Meyers began the news that night by saying, "I'm Seth Meyers—Amy Poehler is not here because she is having a baby."[84] Later in the segment Maya Rudolph and Kenan Thompson sang a special song for her and told her they could not wait to meet her baby. When Poehler watched the touching tribute, she said it made her cry.

Archibald "Archie" William Emerson Arnett made his entrance into the world on October 25, 2008, weighing 8 pounds, 1 ounce (3.6kg). He was named after his father, whose full name is William Emerson Arnett. The elder Arnett fell quickly into his new role as father, even though he admits to being intimidated by the responsibility of having to take care of a vulnerable little person. "But even in its scariest moments it's fantastic," he says. He also admits to being a little overprotective of his son, noting that "if it was socially acceptable I'd be the first one to have my kid in a full helmet and like a cage across his face mask."[85]

Abel James Arnett, the couple's second child, was born on August 6, 2010. With two young children at home and a full work schedule, Poehler and Arnett had to do a lot of juggling and scheduling. "I have, like 15 robots," Poehler once joked to journalist Katie Couric about how the couple made it work. "They do everything from singing lullabies to driving the kids to soccer. It's just amazing what robots can do."[86] In reality, Poehler did have a lot of help with her kids. She says that she feels fortunate that her salary allows her to get the kind of support she needs so she can keep working and still raise a family.

The Cartoon Poehlers

Poehler had at least some experience dealing with children before she had two of her own. She had worked with baby actors on the set of *Baby Mama*. She had also "given birth" to Bessie Higgenbottom, an enthusiastic, bespectacled, gap-toothed 9 ¾-year-old cartoon character. Poehler created the character for the Nickelodeon network series *The Mighty B!*

Poehler created *The Mighty B!* in 2007 with some help from Erik Weise (a storyboard artist who had worked on *SpongeBob SquarePants*) and Cynthia True (a writer from *The Fairly OddParents*). She also provided Bessie's voice. Poehler has described Bessie as "superoptimistic and a super spaz."[87] Bessie was Kaitlin, Stacy, and just about every lisping preteen character Poehler had ever created all rolled up in one, except that she was animated. The character was a tribute to several of her idols. "She's like part Animal from *The Muppets*, part [cartoon character] Daffy Duck, part [folksy actor] Jimmy Stewart, and part Gilda Radner,"[88] Poehler says. The greatest joy in Bessie's life came from being a Honeybee, a fictional version of the Girl Scouts. Poehler says she shares Bessie's bossiness, although she never had much success during her own time as a Girl Scout. "I probably learned to fold a paper bird, and then I think I was done,"[89] she says.

Nickelodeon loved *The Mighty B!* so much that it signed on to air twenty episodes of the show and placed it in its prime Saturday morning time slot. Poehler had high hopes for the show and its main character, beloved to Poehler because Bessie was a

In this 2010 photo, Poehler, pregnant with her second son, enjoys some family time with Arnett and their young son Archie.

unique kid who was not afraid to be girly and tough at the same time. "My dream would be that Bessie would spawn all these open-minded, supremely confident young girls,"[90] Poehler says. Much to Poehler's disappointment, *The Mighty B!* was canceled in 2011, but it did run for nearly four seasons.

Poehler has provided voice talent to several roles, including **Sally O'Malley** *in* **Horton Hears a Who.**

Bessie Higgenbottom is not the only cartoon character to have spouted Poehler's unique voice. She has also lent her vocal talent to characters in several animated movies. In *Shrek the Third* (2007) she was the voice behind Snow White, whom she described as high-strung and stressed out because she had to take care of seven guys. She also played the voices of Sally O'Malley in *Horton Hears a Who* (2008), the computer in *Monsters vs. Aliens* (2009), Eleanor in *Alvin and the Chipmunks: The Squeakquel* (2009) and *Alvin and the Chipmunks: Chipwrecked* (2011), and Gretel in *Hoodwinked Too! Hood vs. Evil* (2011). Finally, in 2012, she played opposite husband Will Arnett as the title character's parents in the Japanese anime movie *The Secret World of Arrietty*.

But back in 2008, before she got involved with any of these projects, Poehler was getting ready to star in a show all her own. Her family was growing, and so was her career. Executives at NBC had big plans for her, which revolved around a brand-new series called *Parks and Recreation*.

Chapter 5

Playing Politics

Amy Poehler had already starred in a successful TV series. She had also made her mark on the big screen and had even played a cartoon character of her own creation. The one thing she had never done was have her own starring role in a project. That was about to change, with a show that was created specifically with her in mind.

Introducing Leslie Knope

After leaving *SNL*, Poehler was looking forward to spending more time with her family. She was also looking to play a character she could spend more time developing than in a single segment of an episode. Several offers came her way, but none felt exactly right.

At around the same time, Michael Schur and Greg Daniels, writer/producers of the hugely successful NBC sitcom *The Office*, were trying to cast a new series they were developing for the same network. It was called *Parks and Recreation*. As with *The Office*, Schur and Daniels sought to create a show in a similar mockumentary, fake-realism style. (In fact, when *Parks and Recreation* first aired, critics complained that it looked and sounded too much like *The Office*.) A mockumentary makes fun of the documentary style, and follows fictitious characters around as they go about their daily business.

Schur had worked with Poehler while he was a writer for *SNL*. He and Daniels believed she was just the right actress to play Leslie Knope, the ambitious deputy director of the Department of Parks and Recreation in the fictional town of Pawnee, Indiana. In fact, Schur wrote the character just for Poehler.

The producers were so confident in Poehler's abilities that they also involved her in casting, producing, and writing the show; in their opinion, she does *everything* well. "If she were just a writer, she'd be the best writer on staff, and if she were just an actress, she'd be the best actress in the cast. And if she were just a mom, she'd be the best mom in America,"[91] Schur says. Leading the writing and producing of the show helped feed Poehler's need to be in charge. "I get a little itchy if I don't have some control,"[92] she says.

The producers thought Poehler had just the right personality for the part. They were sure audiences would fall in love with her friendly smile, not to mention her intelligence and finely tuned comedic abilities. "Amy has a very sharp comedy mind,"

Parks and Recreation was initially slow to find an audience, but soon grew into a comedic success.

Amy Poehler, Diva?

Sometimes, famous women get accused of being a "diva," someone whose fame has instilled in them a sense of entitlement, pickiness, or superiority. A diva might ask for nothing but green M&M's in her dressing room, for example, or demand that a red carpet be rolled out every time she makes an appearance.

By all accounts, Amy Poehler is no diva—she is sweet, down-to-earth, and unassuming. But she is fascinated by the idea of a diva and likes to pretend she is one. "I have, like, 15 different assistants, and I don't know any of their names," she once told Katie Couric in her deadpan style. "I make them print out a sheet that I hand to all my coworkers that says the following: Do not look me in the eye. Do not call me by my first name. Do not call me by my last name. Do not call me. Do not speak unless you're spoken to. You're fired."

Quoted in Katie Couric. "Amy Poehler Tells Katie Couric, 'I Just Love Bossy Women!'" *Glamour*, April 2011. www.glamour.com/sex-love-life/2011/04/amy-poehler-tells-katie-couric-i-just-love-bossy-women?printable=true.

Daniels says. "She's particularly good [at] playing completely deluded characters, so that's what we gave her."[93]

The show centers around Knope, who believes she can change the world. She wants to start by building a park on an old abandoned lot in an attempt to beautify her town; however, government red tape and demanding taxpayers keep getting in her way. It is also hard to focus on her ambitious aims when she has to spend so much time dealing with small-time issues like leash laws and parking meter fines.

Knope is determined to get her park built, even though the odds are against her. The character is not shrewd or cool, but Poehler admires her boundless enthusiasm. "She's one of those people who believe that one person can make a difference; that no matter how small your job is, you still matter."[94]

Actor Rob Lowe and Poehler, as their characters Chris Traeger and Leslie Knope, in a scene from **Parks and Recreation.**

Poehler refers to her character as a "misguided optimist"[95] because Knope so rarely succeeds at her ambitious efforts. Take, for example, an episode in which she imports a pair of penguins so they can be "married" in a special ceremony at the local zoo. What she does not realize is that both penguins are male, and the idea of a gay marriage, even between penguins, outrages many Pawnee residents.

"Leslie tries so hard, but she's not very self-aware,"[96] Poehler says of Knope. For example, Knope has visions of rising from her town's Parks and Recreation Department to become governor, then senator from Indiana, and finally to become the first female president of the United States. In the show's pilot, Knope counts herself among some pretty big-name politicians when she says, "This government isn't just a boy's club anymore. Women are everywhere. It's a great time to be a woman in politics. Hillary

Clinton, Sarah Palin, me."[97] She wants to make it to the big time in government, even though she has no clue how to get there.

Portraying a local politician with big ambitions came naturally to Poehler after playing Hillary Clinton and a cast of other political characters on *SNL*. She also has some personal traits in common with her character. Like Knope, Poehler likes being organized and in charge. She was class secretary and a member of several committees in high school. Yet the two women are also very different. Poehler is much more cynical than the optimistic Knope, and she says she could never have run for public office, although she claims her reasons have nothing to do with politics. "I've been to public buildings and the lighting is so terrible I could not handle it,"[98] she jokes.

Poehler shares another attribute with her character—determination. She started working on *Parks and Recreation* just six weeks after giving birth to her son Archie in 2008. There was very little time to get back to her old self, or to get her body back in shape before jumping into work again.

While Poehler was struggling to lose the pounds she had put on during pregnancy, *Parks and Recreation* was struggling to gain viewers. The ratings were disappointing at first, and the show was almost canceled twice. Finally, in 2011, *Parks and Recreation* found a loyal audience, and Poehler hit her mark. "Every time you start a show, you're at the bottom of Show Mountain," is how Poehler puts it. "Now we're no longer at the bottom. We're climbing. It's a great feeling."[99]

Slowly the accolades for her work started rolling in. She was nominated for two Emmy Awards (for Outstanding Lead Actress and for Writer in a Comedy Series) and a Golden Globe Award (for Best Performance by an Actress in a Television Series—Comedy or Musical). The writers of the show, including Poehler, were also nominated for a Writers Guild of America Award in 2012.

Highlighting the show's popularity, in 2012 Vice President Joe Biden showed up for a cameo performance. Biden played himself in a scene in which he is fawned over by Leslie Knope, who has a big crush on him. Poehler even got to lean in and give the vice president a kiss. "It was really fun," she said. "He was a good sport and a great improviser."[100]

A Most Influential Person

If having a hit show and two healthy children were not enough, in 2011 *Time* magazine named her one of the "100 Most Influential People on the Planet." Poehler's *Parks and Recreation* costar Aziz Ansari wrote the tribute for the magazine. After jokingly scolding Poehler for not returning his phone calls, e-mails, or texts and for convincing him to invest fifteen thousand dollars in a sketchy real estate opportunity, Ansari wrote how much he admires her and the way her work always presents something fresh and unexpected. "I have found that she is as kind and caring a person as she is hilarious," he wrote. "Simply put, Amy Poehler is my hero."[101]

Another honor came when Poehler was asked to give the Class Day speech to seniors at Harvard University in Cambridge, Massachusetts. Harvard is an Ivy League school and is among the top colleges in the country. To make light of the institution's prestige, Poehler began her speech by mentioning one of her sillier movies. "I can only assume I am here today because of my subtle and layered work in a timeless classic called *Deuce Bigalow, Male Gigolo*. And for that I say, 'You're welcome.'"[102] Poehler joked with the students that she wrote her speech just like she wrote every paper when she was in college, by staying up all night and typing it on a word processor.

After cracking a few more jokes, Poehler got serious. She had some important advice to share with the graduating seniors, which she had learned from years of working in the entertainment industry. "You can't do it alone. As you navigate through the rest of your life, be open to collaboration," she said. "Other people and other people's ideas are often better than your own. Find a group of people who challenge and inspire you, spend a lot of time with them, and it will change your life."[103] Poehler's parents proudly listened to her speech from the audience.

Also in 2011, Poehler received *Variety*'s Power of Comedy Award for her many contributions to the world of comedy, from her work with the Upright Citizens Brigade to her starring role on *Parks and Recreation*. Actor Will Ferrell presented her with the award, joking as he made the introduction, "This person is so great . . . and I totally forget their name," he deadpanned.

Poehler says she was honored to speak to graduating seniors at the Harvard Class Day in 2011.

After asking the audience for a hint, Ferrell began lavishing praise on his former *SNL* costar, calling her "one of the great comedians, whether male or female, of our generation."[104]

More praise came from Poehler's husband, Will Arnett, who gave a hilarious tribute in which he spent more time talking about himself than about his wife. Tina Fey and Seth Meyers sent along a video message because they were unable to appear at the event. For not making it to the ceremony, Poehler facetiously called her former *SNL* costars "dead to me."[105] Maya Rudolph did show up, however, and dedicated a very inappropriate but funny R. Kelly song to Poehler.

Giving Back

The awards show was not just a tribute to Poehler. It was also a fund-raiser for the Noreen Fraser Foundation, an organization that supports women's cancer research. For Poehler, doing charity work is an important part of being a celebrity. That is why she regularly takes part in charity events. "Giving back is the ultimate way to get out of yourself and to be of service,"[106] she says.

Just a week before the Power of Comedy award ceremony, she and Arnett cohosted the Worldwide Orphans Foundation's seventh annual benefit gala in New York City. This organization, which provides medical care and other programs for orphans around the world, has a special place in Poehler's heart. She had met its founder, Jane Aronson, in 2009 when they were both honored in the *Glamour* Women of the Year Awards. Since then she has admired Aronson's passion for her cause.

Poehler also appeared in an antibullying public service announcement (PSA) for the Gay & Lesbian Alliance Against Defamation (GLAAD), along with her *Parks and Recreation* costar Rashida Jones. They told viewers, "You have the power to make a difference."[107] Poehler's PSA was part of a series of celebrity ads that took a strong stand against the bullying of lesbian, gay, bisexual, and transgender youths. Other stars in the PSA series included Broadway actress Kristin Chenoweth, former NBA basketball player Shaquille O'Neal, and *Glee* actress Naya Rivera.

Poehler also lent her support to another PSA in 2012, this one supporting reproductive rights for women. In the video, she appears along with other celebrities, such as Meryl Streep, Sarah Silverman, and Kevin Bacon. They speak out against lawmakers who seek to limit women's ability to access birth control and abortion. In it, they encourage women to sign the Bill of Reproductive Rights and urge the U.S. Congress and the president to support women's reproductive rights.

Smart Girls at the Party

In addition to supporting these and other causes, Poehler has created her own project to help young girls grow up into strong women. In *The Mighty B!*'s Bessie Higgenbottom, Poehler created a smart, strong-willed female character whom she hoped preteen girls could relate to. Next she wanted to design a place where these girls could hang out and have fun safely online. The result was the website Smart Girls at the Party. She developed the site together with Meredith Walker, the former head of talent for *SNL*, and Amy Miles, senior producer of the Nickelodeon show *Nick News*. "My goal—my five-year plan—is for it to be the kind of site girls go to when they wake up in the morning,"[108] Poehler says.

Smart Girls at the Party aims to create positive energy by celebrating the unique spirit of every young girl. It encourages girls

Worldwide Orphans Foundation founder and CEO Jane Aronson and Poehler attend the Worldwide Orphans Foundation's annual benefit in 2010.

Pawnee: The Greatest Town in America

Fans of *Parks and Recreation* had something to talk—and read—about in 2011, when the fictitious Leslie Knope released a book chronicling the history of Pawnee, Indiana. *Pawnee: The Greatest Town in America*, was written by Amy Poehler, although she does not admit to it. "I didn't write it, but she [Knope] did let me read it,"[1] she told reporters. According to the book's cover, it was "Written, Compiled, Researched, Typed, Collated, Proofread, and Run through Spell Check"[2] by Leslie Knope. Many of the show's other characters contributed to the book, too.

Although *Pawnee: The Greatest Town in America* was created to promote the show, it chronicles the full history of this fictional town. The City of Pawnee website (www.pawnee indiana.com) recounts some of this history, including how the town's famous church was eventually turned into a linen outlet and how both bread factories in town burned down, turning everything inside them to toast.

Pawnee might not be a real town, and Leslie Knope may just be its fictional Parks and Recreation Department deputy director, but through Poehler's words, Knope's passion for Pawnee feels very real.

1. Quoted in Carol Memmott. "Amy Poehler Dishes About the Book Written by Leslie Knope." *USA Today*, October 2011. www.usatoday.com/life/books/story/2011-10-05/amy-poehler-parks-and-recreation-leslie-knope/50671476/1.
2. Leslie Knope. *Pawnee: The Greatest Town in America*. New York: Universal Studios City Productions, 2011.

to change their world by being themselves. It contains short video episodes in which Poehler interviews young girls about what they like to do and what they want to be when they grow up. At the end of each segment, the music starts and everyone gets up and has a dance party.

The site features profiles and stories of women who have made a powerful impact on the world—from Tammy Duckworth, the first Asian American woman elected to Congress, to nineteenth-century French philosopher and political activist Simone de Beauvoir. The goal is to empower young girls by showing them that they can accomplish anything they set their mind to.

One section of the site allows girls to "Ask Amy" questions, which often deal with the body issues that are so important to teenage girls. Poehler says that if she had had the chance to ask a question to her adult self back when she was a teen, her "question probably would have been like, 'I'm so flat-chested. What do I do about it?' My answer would be like, 'Enjoy it while you can. Being flat-chested is great. Clothes fit and it's amazing.'"[109]

Not everyone was as excited as Poehler about Smart Girls at the Party, however. Alyssa Rosenberg of *Slate* found the web series "disappointing." She thought Poehler did not do enough to draw out the potential in her young interviewees. "Poehler and her producer treat the subjects like they're kids getting a chance to sit at the adult's table for dessert. Acting overly amazed by these girls only plays up their adorableness, rather than presenting them as the future leaders Poehler actually wants them to be,"[110] she wrote. Yet other critics found the teen-focused site worth cheering. The *Huffington Post,* for example, hailed Smart Girls at the Party as one of the "YouTube shows you should be watching."[111]

The Real(ish) Amy Poehler

Getting to know the real Amy Poehler can be difficult when she is constantly delivering one-liners. She frequently responds to interviewers' earnest questions with sarcastic answers or eye-rolling responses (such as when she tried to convince journalist Katie Couric that she was a diva, or *USA Today* reporter Donna Freydkin that she and her husband met over the Jewish dating website J-Date). But every now and then she reveals her real preferences, hobbies, likes, and dislikes.

For someone with such a busy personal and professional schedule, Poehler still makes time to chill out in front of the television. When she does watch TV, surprisingly, Poehler is not a big fan of comedies. She would rather watch old episodes of drama series like *Law and Order*. In fact, she says that if she could only watch one show for the rest of her life, that would be it.

Poehler also finds time to read. She has loved books ever since she was a child. Some of her favorite books are *I Like You* by Amy Sedaris, *Traveling Mercies* by Anne Lamott, and *A Tale of Two Cities* by Charles Dickens.

When it comes to music, Poehler's choices might seem unusual. She says she likes the rap group Bone Thugs N Harmony. She is also a fan of the Adele song, "Someone Like You." And the very first concert she went to was New Edition, an African American boy band from her hometown of Boston. The quintet was popular during the 1980s and helped launch the career of R&B singer Bobby Brown.

One of her favorite pastimes is spending time with sons Archie and Abel. Poehler credits her sons with keeping her grounded in reality when she gets too focused on herself. "Every time I get in my head, my boys are like, 'Hey, hey. Right here. Let's live this moment now, right here,'"[112] she says.

Turning Forty and Looking Forward

In 2011 Amy Poehler turned forty, a major milestone. Like many women, she was not looking forward to the occasion. "Oh my god, I hate birthdays," she said. "I never celebrate them. I have no interest."[113] Though Poehler has not relied on her looks like other actresses have, turning middle-aged in the entertainment industry, where looks are everything, can pose challenges to any woman's career, even a comedian's. Once women reach their forties and beyond, they sometimes stop getting offered leading roles. They are typically relegated to playing the mother, or even the grandmother, of the lead actress.

Besides turning forty, Poehler faced another challenge in 2012. In September of that year, she and Arnett announced that they were separating after nine years of marriage. Although the couple did not offer any details about the reasons for their split, they described it as a friendly separation. In fact, the media seemed to be more distraught than the couple, at least in part

As a busy working mom and actress/producer, Poehler says she loves spending her downtime with her children.

because Arnett and Poehler had seemed like the perfect pair. *Yahoo! Canada* ran a headline that read, "Amy Poehler, Will Arnett Split; Hope Dies." The author of the post despaired over the breakup because "we innocently thought that Poehler and Arnett had a real shot at making it. After all, their union seemed like it was made in TV comedy heaven."[114] Fan Hadley Freeman tweeted, "I feel like my best friends have broken up. Saddest celebrity split ever."[115]

Through the divorce, both Poehler and Arnett were committed to keeping a sense of normalcy for their two young sons.

"They both understand that things are different, but they're easing into the situation. Amy is doing everything to keep them protected,"[116] a source close to the couple told reporters. Spending time with her boys helped take Poehler's mind off her personal struggles.

"That Petite Comedic Mastermind"

Despite this personal setback, Poehler's career showed no signs of slowing down. In the spring of 2012, she had just wrapped the fourth season of *Parks and Recreation*. At the Emmy Awards in September of that year, she was nominated for both Outstanding Lead Actress in a Comedy and Outstanding Writing for a Comedy. Though she did not win either award (she lost the acting award to Julia Louis-Dreyfus for the HBO series *Veep* and the writing award to comedian Louis C.K. for the show *Louie*), Poehler did have some memorable moments at the awards ceremony.

On the red carpet, she boasted to interviewer Ryan Seacrest that instead of opting for the expensive baubles most celebrities flaunt at the Emmys, she wore a ring that cost two dollars and came out of her sons' toy box. Later during the show, as Louis-Dreyfus started to read her acceptance speech for the Outstanding Lead Actress award, it was obvious something was amiss, as she read, "First of all, I would like to thank NBC, *Parks and Rec*, my beautiful boys Archie and Abel. . . . " The camera cut to Poehler in the audience, who was looking at a piece of paper in her hand. It was obvious from her expression that the two actresses had intentionally switched speeches as a joke. Poehler ran to the stage to give Louis-Dreyfus the correct speech. At the end of the speech, Louis-Dreyfus read something that had been written at the bottom of the page: "Isn't it a shame that Amy Poehler didn't win? What?"[117] The camera cut to Poehler in the audience, a pencil raised in her hand as if she had sneakily added the note to Louis-Dreyfus' speech. Some reviewers considered the speech switch one of the most memorable moments in that year's awards show. "Basically, Poehler—that petite, comedic mastermind—managed to make this her Emmy moment even though she didn't even *win the thing*,"[118] pointed out one blogger.

Also in 2012 Poehler announced that she would produce a new show for Comedy Central. She convinced the network to pick up *Broad City*, a web series starring actresses Abbi Jacobson and Ilana Glazer as two women trying to navigate through the trials and tribulations of everyday life in New York City. "Amy

Poehler and actress Julia Louis-Dreyfus (with statue) have a little fun at the 2012 Emmy Awards ceremony.

Teaming with her good friend Tina Fey to host the 2013 Golden Globe Awards proved a huge success for Poehler.

Poehler told me this would be a great show for us, and that's good enough for me,"[119] says Comedy Central's head of original programming, Kent Alterman. It was a testament to just how far Poehler's star had risen. Back in the 1990s, she and the other cast members of the Upright Citizens Brigade had to practically beg the network to pick up their show. Now, Poehler was influencing Comedy Central's programming decisions.

There were also more partnerships ahead with friend and fellow comedic actress Fey. They appeared together on the Comedy Central charity event "Night of Too Many Stars," which raised money for autism awareness. During the show, the two women auctioned off the chance to be their best friend. Two women in the audience jumped at the chance, bidding forty-six thousand dollars each for the opportunity to hang out backstage with Poehler and Fey for a few hours.

Fey and Poehler also hosted the Golden Globe Awards in January 2013. For the previous three years, British comedian Ricky Gervais had hosted this annual awards show, in which the Hollywood Foreign Press Association honors the best television shows and movies. Paul Telegdy, president of NBC Entertainment's alternative and late-night programming called the hiring of Fey and Poehler as hosts "a major coup. . . . Tina and Amy have a proven chemistry and comedic timing from their many years together on *SNL* to their successful co-starring roles in *Baby Mama*."[120] It was the first time the show had female co-hosts. Their performance was the night's big winner. One reviewer wrote, "It took them only seven minutes at the start of the show to leave legions of previous awards show hosts in the dust."[121] The duo earned rave reviews by poking fun at Hollywood's elite, like this jab from Poehler: "The Golden Globes, where the beautiful people of film rub shoulders with the rat-faced people of television."[122]

The Future of Poehler

Whatever her career has in store for her, Poehler remains optimistic. Just like the girls she encourages with Smart Girls at the Party and her cartoon alter-ego Bessie Higgenbottom, Poehler believes the sky is the limit. She can do anything she chooses to do. When one reporter asked what her future might hold, Poehler replied with her usual sense of humor, "Maybe I'll breed pigeons, open a school, fly a solid gold plane, or I'll go 'green'—but I'll go dark green, I won't use paper, I'll write an entire screenplay in sand on the beach."[123] Whatever she does, her future seems full of possibilities, all of them funny.

Introduction: Changing the Course of Comedy

1. Quoted in Sloane Crosley. "Amy Poehler: The Entertainer." *Glamour*, November 3, 2009. www.glamour.com/inspired /women-of-the-year/2009/amy-poehler.
2. *Saturday Night Live*. "Update: Palin Rap," October 18, 2008. www.hulu.com/watch/39808/saturday-night-live-update -palin-rap.
3. Quoted in Kera Bolonik. "Welcome to Her Island." *New York*, May 15, 2011. http://nymag.com/print/?/arts/tv/up fronts/2011/amy-poehler-2011-5/.

Chapter 1: Boston Born and Bred

4. Quoted in Joseph P. Kahn. "Chasing Amy." *Boston Globe*, May 5, 2006, p. D3.
5. Quoted in Nancie Clare. "Q + LA: Amy Poehler." *Los Angeles Times Magazine*, January 2011. www.latimesmagazine .com/2011/01/q-la-amy-poehler.html.
6. Quoted in Alex Strachan. "'More Nope, Less Dope'; Amy Poehler Goes Off-Script with Alex Strachan About Her Time on *Parks & Recreation*." *Ottawa Citizen* (Ontario, Canada), April 15, 2010, p. E8.
7. *Saturday Night Live*. "Amy's Bedroom," October 13, 2007. www.hulu.com/watch/1586/saturday-night-live-amys -bedroom.
8. Quoted in Stephen Sherrill. "Meet the Parents: The Poehlers." *Wall Street Journal*, February 25, 2011.
9. Quoted in Ashley Van Buren. "Amy Poehler: The Smartest Girl at the *New Yorker* Festival," Mediaite, October 3, 2011. www.mediaite.com/online/amy-poehler-the-smartest-girl -at-the-new-yorker-festival/.
10. Quoted in Lindsey Cardarelli. "Burlington's Amy Poehler Brings Local Laughs. *Woburn (MA) Daily Chronicle*, November 1, 2005. www.woburnonline.com/frontpage /november05/11105-4.html.

11. Quoted in Molly Lopez. "Amy Poehler." *People*, May 5, 2008. www.people.com/people/archive/article/0,,20196082,00 .html.
12. Quoted in Sherrill. "Meet the Parents."
13. Quoted in Bolonik. "Welcome to Her Island."
14. *Inside the Actor's Studio.* "Women in Comedy: Amy Poehler." www.hulu.com/watch/95891/inside-the-actors-studio -amy-poehler-women-in-comedy.
15. Quoted in *Burlington County (MA) Times.* "As a Child, Amy Poehler Loved Fairy Tales . . . ," May 12, 2007, p. B6.
16. Quoted in Kahn. "Chasing Amy," p. D3.
17. Quoted in Sherrill. "Meet the Parents."
18. Quoted in Crystal G. Martin. "Amy Poehler's Aha! Moment." Oprah.com, February 16, 2011. www.oprah.com /spirit/Amy-Poehler-on-Her-Aha-Moment.
19. Quoted in Elizabeth Gehrman. "Free Play." *Boston College Magazine*, Winter 2005. http://bcm.bc.edu/issues /winter_2005/images/fleabag.pdf.
20. Quoted in Sherrill. "Meet the Parents."

Chapter 2: An Upright Citizen

21. Quoted in Brian Raftery. "And . . . Scene." *New York*, September 25, 2011. http://nymag.com/print/?/arts/comics/ features/upright-citizens-brigade-2011-10/.
22. Quoted in "Possible SiDe EfFeCtS—An Interview with Amy Poehler." www.andrew.cmu.edu/user/ott/resources/0000 _poehler.html.
23. Quoted in Nathan Rabin. "Interview Amy Poehler." A.V. Club, March 31, 2008. www.avclub.com/articles/amy -poehler,14220/.
24. Quoted in Erik Pedersen. "Tina Fey and Amy Poehler: Almost Married?" *E Online*, April 23, 2008. www.eonline .com/news/tina_fey_amy_poehler_almost_married/345.
25. Quoted in Reed Tucker. "The Girlie Show!" *New York Post*, October 17, 2012. www.nypost.com/p/entertainment/the _girlie_show_ts2NhPzkYn9fng8TkW6XeJ.
26. Quoted in Tucker. "The Girlie Show!"
27. Quoted in Raftery. "And . . . Scene."

28. Quoted in Michael Ordoña. "Amy Poehler Talks of Upright Citizens Brigade," *San Francisco Chronicle*, January 8, 2012. www.sfgate.com/cgi-bin/article.cgi?f=/c/a/2012/01/06/PK5D1MHBMC.DTL&ao=all.
29. Quoted in Raftery. "And . . . Scene."
30. Quoted in Raftery. "And . . . Scene."
31. Quoted in Raftery. "And . . . Scene."
32. Quoted on YouTube. "UCB on Rock Center." www.youtube.com/watch?v=en8Z72ZIq9Y.
33. Quoted in Clare. "Q + LA: Amy Poehler."
34. Quoted in Paul Brownfield. "Upright Citizens Brigade Spins Chaos into Comedy." *Los Angeles Times*, August 19, 1998. http://articles.latimes.com/1998/aug/19/entertainment/ca-14365.
35. YouTube. "Upright Citizens Brigade, Season 3, Episode 3." www.youtube.com/watch?v=PtNGjqyakak&feature=related.
36. YouTube. "Upright Citizens Brigade, Season 3, Episode 3."
37. Quoted in Nick Zaino. "Outside 'SNL,' Poehler Stays Edgy with Improv." *Boston Globe*, October 31, 2003, p. C16.
38. Quoted in Ordoña. "Amy Poehler Talks of Upright Citizens Brigade."
39. Quoted in Zaino. "Outside 'SNL,' Poehler Stays Edgy with Improv," p. C16.
40. Quoted in Raftery. "And . . . Scene."
41. Quoted in Ordoña. "Amy Poehler Talks of Upright Citizens Brigade."

Chapter 3: Live from New York!

42. Quoted in Andrew Ryan. "Poehler for President." *Globe and Mail* (Toronto), April 6, 2009, p. R1.
43. Quoted in CNN.com. "Cast of 'Saturday Night Live' Speaks," September 24, 2010. http://transcripts.cnn.com/TRANSCRIPTS/1009/24/lkl.01.html.
44. Quoted in Dave Itzkoff. "Please Don't Tell Her She's Funny for a Girl." *New York Times*, March 18, 2007.
45. Quoted in Joshua Alston. "Poehler's Opposites." *Newsweek*, March 26, 2009. www.thedailybeast.com/newsweek/2009/03/26/poehler-s-opposites.html.

46. NBC.com. "Reese Witherspoon Monologue." www.nbc
com/saturday-night-live/video/reese-witherspoon-mono
logue/1349560/.

47. Tina Fey. *Bossypants*. New York: Hachette Audio, 2011.

48. Aly Semigran. "Kristen Wiig Is Amongst 'Top Three or
Four' 'Saturday Night Live' Performers, says Lorne Michaels. Do You Agree?" *Entertainment Weekly*, April 29,
2011. http://popwatch.ew.com/2011/04/29/kristen-wiig
-lorne-michaels-top-snl-cast-member/.

49. Quoted in Erin Overbey. "The Tina Fey Years." *New Yorker*,
March 7, 2011. www.newyorker.com/online/blogs/backis
sues/2011/03/saturday-night-live.html.

50. Quoted in Itzkoff. "Please Don't Tell Her She's Funny for
a Girl."

51. Quoted in Alston. "Poehler's Opposites."

52. Quoted in National Public Radio. "For Amy Poehler,
Comedy Is a Walk in the 'Park,' September 18, 2009. www
.npr.org/templates/story/story.php?storyId=112961878.

53. Quoted in CNN.com. "Live from New York, It's Hillary
Clinton." http://edition.cnn.com/2008/POLITICS/03/01
/clinton.snl/.

54. NBC.com. "Palin/Hillary Open." www.nbc.com/saturday
-night-live/video/palin-hillary-open/656281/.

55. Quoted in Danny Shea. "Amy Poehler Leaving 'Saturday
Night Live' After Election." *Huffington Post*, September
16, 2008. www.huffingtonpost.com/2008/09/16/amy
-poehler-leaving-satur_n_126841.html.

56. Quoted in Lauren A.E. Schuker. "Going for Belly Laughs;
'Saturday Night Live's' Amy Poehler Finds She's in Demand
All Week," *Wall Street Journal*, April 19, 2008, p. W1.

57. Fey. *Bossypants*.

58. Quoted in Donna Freydkin. "Arnett & Poehler Sittin' in a
Tree L-a-u-g-h-i-n-g." *USA Today*, March 23, 2007, p. E1.

59. Quoted in Randy Kennedy. "A First for Fake News."
New York Times, October 12, 2004. www.nytimes.com
/2004/10/12/arts/television/12nbc.html.

60. Quoted in Kennedy. "A First for Fake News."

61. NBC.com. "Really!?!: Gov. Blagojevich." www.nbc.com /saturday-night-live/video/really-gov-blagojevich/881482/.

62. Quoted in Jennifer Holton and Bob Seeholzer. "The CN's Exlusive Interview with Seth Meyers," February 25, 2010. www.jcunews.com/2010/02/25/seth-meyers/.

63. *Saturday Night Live*. "Weekend Update: Amy's Good-bye." www.hulu.com/watch/48722/saturday-night-live-update -amys-goodbye.

64. Quoted in David Carr. "The Hemi Q&A: Amy Poehler." *Hemispheres Inflight Magazine*, December 1, 2011. www .hemispheresmagazine.com/2011/12/01/the-hemi-qa -amy-poehler/.

Chapter 4: *Baby Mama*

65. YouTube. "*Baby Mama*—Film Clip #5." www.youtube .com/watch?v=Wupd5pRxZKY.

66. YouTube. "Peeing in the Sink." www.youtube.com/watch ?v=NBndUyf1jfY.

67. Paul Brownfield. "Tina Fey and Amy Poehler Gamble with the Gal-Pal Comedy 'Baby Mama.'" *Los Angeles Times*, April 20, 2008. http://articles.latimes.com/2008/apr/20/enter tainment/ca-feypoehler20.

68. Quoted in Kristen Baldwin. "Tina Fey: One Hot 'Mama.'" *Entertainment Weekly*, April 9, 2008. www.ew.com/ew/ar ticle/0,,20190281_5,00.html.

69. Manohla Dargis. "Learning on the Job About Birthing Ba-bies." *New York Times*, April 25, 2008. http://movies.ny times.com/2008/04/25/movies/25baby.html.

70. Stephanie Zacharek. "*Baby Mama*." *Salon*, April 23, 2008. www.salon.com/ent/movies/review/2008/04/23/baby _mama/.

71. Claudia Puig. "'Baby Mama' Brings Funny to Full Term." *USA Today*, April 25, 2008. www.usatoday.com/life /movies/reviews/2008-04-24-baby-mama_N.htm.

72. Wesley Morris. "A Bundle of Laughs from Two Funny Women." *Boston Globe*, April 25, 2008. www.boston.com /movies/display?display=movie&id=10726.

73. Dargis. "Learning on the Job About Birthing Babies."

74. Quoted in Glenn Whipp. "Pregnant Pause Tina Fey, Amy Poehler and Life on the Mommy Track." *Los Angeles Daily News*, April 25, 2008, p. L1.

75. Quoted in Pauline O'Connor. "A Night Out with Amy Poehler: Live from New York." *New York Times*, April 4, 2004. www.nytimes.com/2004/04/04/fashion/04NITE .html?ex=1085025600&en=fdd090f31460f590&ei=5070.

76. Quoted in Freydkin. "Arnett & Poehler Sittin' in a Tree L-a-u-g-h-i-n-g," p. E1.

77. Quoted in Freydkin. "Arnett & Poehler Sittin' in a Tree L-a-u-g-h-i-n-g," p. E1.

78. Quoted in Freydkin. "Arnett & Poehler Sittin' in a Tree L-a-u-g-h-i-n-g," p. E1.

79. Quoted in Reed Tucker. "Hot Seat—Will Arnett & Amy Poehler." *New York Post*, March 25, 2007.

80. Quoted in Carr. "The Hemi Q&A: Amy Poehler."

81. Quoted in Tucker. "Hot Seat," p. 032.

82. Quoted in Donna Freydkin. "Emmy Spotlight: Poehler's Pregnant, Not Pausing." *USA Today*, September 18, 2008. www.usatoday.com/life/television/televisionawards /emmys/2008-09-17-amy-poehler_N.htm.

83. Quoted in Freydkin. "Emmy Spotlight."

84. Quoted in Rachel Sklar. "Amy Poehler Has Baby Boy—But SNL Sadness as She Leaves the Show." *Huffington Post*, November 25, 2008. www.huffingtonpost.com/2008/10/25 /a-baby-boy-for-poehler-ba_n_137060.html.

85. Quoted in Nicki Gostin. "Will Arnett Talks Baby Helmets, 'Arrested' Secrets and Loving Conan." PopEater.com, January 22, 2010. www.popeater.com/2010/01/22/will-ar nett-interview/.

86. Quoted in Katie Couric. "Amy Poehler Tells Katie Couric, 'I Just Love Bossy Women!'" *Glamour*, April 2011. www .glamour.com/sex-love-life/2011/04/amy-poehler-tells -katie-couric-i-just-love-bossy-women?printable=true.

87. Quoted in Itzkoff. "Please Don't Tell Her She's Funny for a Girl."

88. Quoted in Matea Gold. "Early Shift for Amy Poehler; the 'SNL' Star Aims to Connect with Kids as a Voice for Nick's

New 'The Mighty B!' Show." *Los Angeles Times*, April 25, 2008, p. E24.

89. Quoted in Gold. "Early Shift for Amy Poehler," p. E24.
90. Quoted in Gold. "Early Shift for Amy Poehler," p. E24.

Chapter 5: Playing Politics

91. Quoted in Bolonik. "Welcome to Her Island."
92. Quoted in Couric. "Amy Poehler Tells Katie Couric, 'I Just Love Bossy Women!'"
93. Quoted in Ryan. "Poehler for President," p. R1.
94. Quoted in Couric. "Amy Poehler Tells Katie Couric, 'I Just Love Bossy Women!'"
95. Quoted in National Public Radio. "For Amy Poehler, Comedy Is a Walk in the 'Park.'"
96. Quoted in Ryan. "Poehler for President," p. R1.
97. Quoted in Linda Holmes. "Amy Poehler: Playing Politics, but Only on Television," *Monkey See* (blog), National Public Radio, October 20, 2011. www.npr.org/blogs/mon keysee/2011/10/20/141533202/amy-poehler-playing-poli tics-but-only-on-television.
98. Quoted in Couric. "Amy Poehler Tells Katie Couric, 'I Just Love Bossy Women!'"
99. Quoted in Carr. "The Hemi Q&A: Amy Poehler."
100. Quoted in Alex Moaba. "Amy Poehler Reminisces About Joe Biden's 'Parks and Recreation' Cameo on 'Live with Kelly and Michael.' *Huffington Post*, November 20, 2012. www.huffingtonpost.com/2012/11/20/amy-poehler-joe -biden_n_2166346.html.
101. Aziz Ansari. "Amy Poehler. *Time*, April 21, 2011. www.time.com/time/specials/packages/article/0,28 804,2066367_2066369_2066436,00.html.
102. Amy Poehler. "Harvard University 2011 Class Day Speech," June 7, 2011. www.youtube.com/watch?v=7 WvdxgGpNVU.
103. Poehler. "Harvard University 2011 Class Day Speech."
104. Eonline.com. "Watch the Funniest Moments from *Variety's* Power of Comedy: Will Ferrell, Amy Poehler, Will Arnett & More!" www.eonline.com/news/276286/watch-the-fun

niest-moments-from-variety-s-power-of-comedy-will-fer
rell-amy-poehler-will-arnett-more.

105. Quoted in Matt Donnelly. "Amy Poehler: Tina Fey and
Seth Meyers Are Dead to Me." *LA Times*, November 21,
2011. http://latimesblogs.latimes.com/gossip/2011/11
/amy-poehler-variety-power-of-comedy-tina-fey-maya-ru
dolph.html.

106. Quoted in Valerie Nome. "Red Carpet Confidential: How
Amy Poehler Bounced Back from Split with Will Arnett."
OK!, November 14, 2012. www.okmagazine.com/blogs
/red-carpet-confidential-how-amy-poehler-bounced-back
-split-will-arnett.

107. Quoted in GLAAD. "Amplify Your Voice." www.glaad.org
/resources/amplifyyourvoice/psa/press.

108. Quoted in Clare. "Q + LA: Amy Poehler."

109. Quoted in David Wright. "Amy Poehler Reaches Out to
Teen Girls with Website, Advice Column." ABC News,
October 19, 2012. http://abcnews.go.com/blogs/enter
tainment/2012/10/amy-poehler-reaches-out-to-teen-girls
-with-website-advice-column/.

110. Alyssa Rosenberg. "Amy Poehler's *Smart Girls at the Party*
Isn't Smart Enough." *Slate*, July 11, 2012. www.slate.com
/blogs/xx_factor/2012/07/11/amy_poehler_and_smart
_girls_at_the_party_web_series_disappoints.html.

111. Jake Coyle. "Amy Poehler's 'Smart Girls at The Party'
& Other YouTube Shows You Should Be Watching,"
Huffington Post, August 7, 2012. www.huffingtonpost
.com/2012/08/07/amy-poehlers-smart-girls-_n_1751227
.html.

112. Quoted in Wright. "Amy Poehler Reaches Out to Teen
Girls with Website, Advice Column."

113. Quoted in Glenn Whipp. "Shhhhh: Poehler Will Be 40."
Los Angeles Times, June 9, 2011, p. S1.

114. Dave Nemetz. "Amy Poehler and Will Arnett Separate:
Why We're So Bummed." *Yahoo! Canada*, September 6,
2012. http://ca.news.yahoo.com/amy-poehler-and-will
-arnett-separate--why-we-re-so-bummed.html.

115. Quoted in Julie Miller. "The Internet Is Crushed Over Amy Poehler and Will Arnett's Separation, May Need Counseling." *Vanity Fair*, September 7, 2012. www.vanityfair.com/online/oscars/2012/09/amy-poehler-will-arnett-separate-internet-grief.

116. Quoted in Christina Stiehl. "Amy Poehler's Sons Are Helping Her Through Divorce." *Hollywood Life*, November 4, 2012. http://hollywoodlife.com/2012/11/04/amy-poehler-divorce-sons-archie-abel/.

117. YouTube. "64th Emmy Awards: Julia Louis-Dreyfus." www.youtube.com/watch?v=vL6Oh2qv9Mo.

118. Jen Chaney. "Emmys 2012: When Julia Louis-Dreyfus Wins, Amy Poehler Wins Also." *Celebritology* (blog), *Washington Post*, September 23, 2012. www.washingtonpost.com/blogs/celebritology/post/emmys-2012-when-julia-louis-dreyfus-wins-amy-poehler-wins-also/2012/09/23/ff797ba8-05e7-11e2-afff-d6c7f20a83bf_blog.html.

119. Quoted in Nellie Andreeva. "Amy Poehler to Produce Comedy Central Pilot Based on 'Broad City' Web Series." *Deadline*, October 8, 2012. www.deadline.com/2012/10/amy-poehler-produced-comedy-based-on-broad-city-web-series-gets-pilot-order-at-comedy-central/.

120. Quoted in *Us Weekly*. "Tina Fey, Amy Poehler to Co-Host 2014 Golden Globes!" October 15, 2012. www.usmagazine.com/entertainment/news/tina-fey-amy-poehler-to-co-host-2013-golden-globes-20121510.

121. Don Kaplan. "Golden Globe Awards 2013: Tina Fey and Amy Poehler Shine as Hosts." *New York Daily News*, January 14, 2013. http://www.nydailynews.com/entertainment/tv-movies/fey-amy-poehler-shine-globes-hosts-article-1.1239605.

122. Quoted in Kaplan. "Golden Globe Awards 2013: Tina Fey and Amy Poehler Shine as Hosts."

123. Quoted in Schuker. "Going for Belly Laughs," p. W1.

1971

Amy Meredith Poehler is born in Burlington, Massachusetts, on September 16.

1989

Poehler graduates from Burlington High School.

1993

Poehler graduates from Boston College and moves to Chicago to study improv.

1995

Poehler joins the Upright Citizens Brigade (UCB) sketch-comedy group.

1996

UCB moves to New York in search of bigger venues and a wider audience.

The Upright Citizens Brigade Theatre opens on West Twenty-Second Street in New York on February 4.

1998

Comedy Central picks up the *Upright Citizens Brigade* sketch-comedy show, which it airs on Wednesday nights at 10:30 P.M.

2000

Comedy Central cancels *Upright Citizens Brigade*.

2001

On September 29 Poehler makes her debut as a featured player on *Saturday Night Live*, just weeks after the September 11 terrorist attacks on New York City and Washington.

2001

Poehler is promoted to a full cast member on *SNL* during her first season, a feat that only Eddie Murphy and Harry Shearer had accomplished before her.

2002

The UCB Theatre is shut down for a fire-code violation, leaving the four-member group without a venue.

2003

UCB opens a 150-seat theater on West Twenty-Sixth Street in New York. The group performs there and teaches improv comedy to young hopefuls.

2003

Poehler marries Canadian actor/comedian Will Arnett.

2004

Poehler and friend/*SNL* colleague Tina Fey become the first all-female anchors to host the recurring *SNL* segment "Weekend Update."

2008

Poehler is nominated for an Outstanding Supporting Actress in a Comedy Emmy, the first time an *SNL* cast member has ever been nominated for this award. It is also when she leaves *SNL*.

Poehler gives birth to son Archibald "Archie" William Emerson Arnett on October 25.

2009

Parks and Recreation, starring Poehler, premieres on NBC on April 9.

2010

Poehler and Arnett welcome their second son, Abel James on August 6.

2011

Time magazine names Poehler one of the "100 Most Influential People on the Planet." She also receives the *Variety* Power of Comedy Award.

2012

Poehler and husband Will Arnett announce that they are divorcing after nine years of marriage.

2013

Poehler and Fey cohost the Golden Globe Awards on January 13.

Books

Bob Bedore. *101 Improv Games for Children and Adults.* Alameda, CA: Hunter House, 2004. In this educational book, kids can learn many of the same improv tricks Amy Poehler and other actors tried when they were studying improvisational comedy.

Leslie Knope. *Pawnee: The Greatest Town in America.* New York: Hyperion, 2011. This is a "historical" look at the fictional town of Pawnee, Indiana, through the eyes of its deputy director of parks and recreation, Leslie Knope, aka Amy Poehler.

Dana Rasmussen. *Funny Girl.* Vol. 2: *Amy Poehler.* Webster's Digital Services, 2010. http://isbndb.com/d/publisher/web sters_digital_services.html. This e-book is a collection of Internet articles chronicling Amy Poehler's career from her time on *Saturday Night Live* to films such as *Baby Mama* and *Mean Girls.*

Jim Whalley. *"Saturday Night Live," Hollywood Comedy, and American Culture.* Hampshire, UK: Palgrave Macmillan, 2010. This book, which is written by a film studies teacher, looks at the ways in which *Saturday Night Live's* influence spilled over into movies such as *Ghostbusters* and *National Lampoon's Animal House.*

Periodicals

Joshua Alston. "Poehler-ized." *Los Angeles Daily Herald*, April 4, 2009.

Aziz Ansari. "Amy Poehler." *Time*, April 21, 2011.

Burlington County (MA) Times. "As a Child, Amy Poehler Loved Fairy Tales . . . ," May 12, 2007.

David Carr. "The Hemi Q&A: Amy Poehler." *Hemispheres Inflight Magazine*, December 1, 2011.

Nancie Clare. "Q + LA: Amy Poehler." *Los Angeles Times Magazine*, January 2011.

Katie Couric. "Amy Poehler Tells Katie Couric, 'I Just Love Bossy Women!'" *Glamour*, April 2011.

Donna Freydkin. "Arnett & Poehler Sittin' in a Tree L-a-u-g-h-i-n-g; 'Glory' Stars' Marriage Is Anything but Icy." *USA Today*, March 23, 2007.

Matea Gold. "Early Shift for Amy Poehler; the 'SNL' Star Aims to Connect with Kids as a Voice for Nick's New 'The Mighty B!' Show." *Los Angeles Times*, April 25, 2008.

Dave Itzkoff. "Please Don't Tell Her She's Funny for a Girl." *New York Times*, March 18, 2007.

Joseph P. Kahn. "Chasing Amy." *Boston Globe*, May 5, 2006.

Cristina Kinon. "Poehler Casts Wide 'Net for 'Smart Girls,'" *New York Daily News*, January 22, 2009.

Michael Ordoña. "Amy Poehler Talks of Upright Citizens Brigade." *San Francisco Chronicle*, January 8, 2012.

Brian Raftery. "And . . . Scene." *New York*, September 25, 2011.

Andrew Ryan. "Poehler for President." *Globe and Mail* (Toronto), April 6, 2009.

Glenn Whipp. "Shhhhh: Poehler Will Be 40." *Los Angeles Times*, June 9, 2011.

Websites

NBC.com (www.nbc.com). NBC is home to both of Poehler's biggest projects—*Parks and Recreation* and *Saturday Night Live*.

Pawnee Indiana.com (www.pawneeindiana.com). The "official" website of the Parks and Recreation Department for the fictional town portrayed on *Parks and Recreation*.

Smart Girls at the Party (www.smartgirlsattheparty.com). Poehler's website, where preteen girls can celebrate what makes them special and bop along with a dance party.

Upright Citizens.org (www.uprightcitizens.org). The comedy troupe where Poehler got her start has a website with information about its performances and classes.

Picture Credits

Cover: © Â RD/Kabik/Retna Ltd./Corbis

© Adam Nemser-PHOTOlink.net/PHOTOlink/Newscom, 12

© AP Images/Liam McMullan, 31

© Blue Sky/20th Century Fox/The Kobal Collection/Art Resource, NY, 60

© Broadway Video/KC Bailey/The Kobal Collection/Art Resource, NY, 51

© Broadway Video/The Kobal Collection/Art Resource, NY, 49

© Christopher Peterson/BuzzFoto/FilmMagic/Getty Images, 59

© Dana Edelson/NBC/NBCU Photo Bank via Getty Images, 9, 37, 39, 40, 45

© Dreamworks/Suzanne Hanover/The Kobal Collection/Art Resource, NY, 55

© Gary Gershoff/WireImage/Getty Images, 27

© Jeff Kravitz/FilmMagic/Getty Images, 46

© John M. Heller/Getty Images, 69

© Kevin Winter/Getty Images, 7, 75

© Mary Ellen Matthews/NBC/NBCU Photo Bank via Getty Images, 35

© M. Caulfield/WireImage/Getty Images, 24

© NBC/Mitchell Haaseth/Photofest, 62

© NBC/NBCU Photo Bank via Getty Images, 18

© NBC-TV/The Kobal Collection/Art Resource, NY, 64

© Paramount/Michael Gibson/The Kobal Collection/Art Resource, NY, 53

© Paul Drinkwater/NBCUniversal via Getty Images, 76

© Photofest, 23

© Rick Friedman/Corbis, 20, 67

© Splash News/Newscom, 14, 17

© Survivor, PacificCoastNews/Newscom, 73

Stephanie Watson is a writer and editor who lives in Providence, Rhode Island, with her husband and son. She has been writing young-adult nonfiction for the better part of a decade, and over that time has written several celebrity bios, including *Heath Ledger: Talented Actor*, *Daniel Radcliffe: Film and Stage Star*, and *The Earnhardt NASCAR Dynasty: The Legacy of Dale Sr. and Dale Jr.* Watson has also contributed many articles to websites such as WebMD and HowStuffWorks. In her free time, she enjoys doing charity work and traveling with her family.